After 50 Years:
The Promised Land is Still Too Far!
1961 - 2011

PUBLISHED BY
Mkuki na Nyota Publishers Ltd
Nyerere Road, Quality Plaza Building
P. O. Box 4246
Dar es Salaam, Tanzania
www.mkukinanyota.com
publish@mkukinanyota.com

© I. Werrema, 2012

ISBN 978-9987-08-170-7

All rights reserved. No part of this publication may be reproduced, stored in a retrieval system or transmitted in any form or by any means, electronic, mechanical, photocopying, recording, or otherwise except for short quotes properly made for academic and professional references, without the prior permission of the Mkuki na Nyota Pulishers.

This book is sold subject to the condition that it should not by way of trade or otherwise be lent, re-sold, hire out or otherwise circulated without the publisher's prior consent in any form of binding or cover other than that in which it is published and without a similar condition including this condition being imposed on the subsequent purchaser.

After 50 Years:
The Promised Land is Still Too Far!
1961 - 2011

Ibrahim Werrema John

Edited by:
Warren D.M. Reed, Jenerali Ulimwengu
and Lisa Smith Holtz

MKUKI NA NYOTA
DAR-ES-SALAAM

Dedicated to:

*My parents, Mr. and Mrs. John I. Keraryo:
who instilled in me a deep love for learning and taught
me what really matters in life*

*My wife:
who has loved me for what I am and gave me the
opportunity to love her*

Contents

Acknowledgements vii

Foreword ix

Introduction xi

The Country 1

Former Presidents 7

Social Services 39

Economy 88

Culture and Religion. 112

Political Situation 121

The New Era 144

Bibliography 163

Acknowledgements

A book is usually the final stage of a long process. I am not an island. I did not do it all alone. Many things were done on my behalf by my friends and relatives. Therefore, a great magnitude of gratitude is owed to the great team I had on board with me in my earlier work, and again in this updated project:

My lovely wife, Agatha, made an incredible contribution. She has demonstrated that she possesses a remarkable level of patience and has been of invaluable assistance to me through her constant advice which I greatly acknowledge and appreciate. I love and I really am proud of her.

A good measure of gratitude is also reserved for my father, John I. Keraryo, an awesome man for whom I have great love and respect. His contribution did not begin with the writing of books. It is historic. There is hardly an English word that I would claim to have known if it were not for my father's tireless efforts to see that I knew not only writing and reading but writing and reading the best I could.

Every time I put together a little piece of information, I remember those "bad" old days when we used to sit around the dining table seeking for something whose meaning I never comprehended then, but of which I do now. I am really proud of my dad who instilled in me a deep love for learning, and who has borne more than just a father-to-son responsibility. He has contributed significantly to my works and my life in general. I thank my dad for the encouragement, advice, and everything that made yet this book a reality.

My mother, Mrs. Elizabeth J. Keraryo, is a wonderful mom. Her contribution has been more inspirational and emotional. She encouraged and advised me. There is no amount of thanks that can measure up to my parents' part in my life for teaching me more powerfully, not in their words, but in their deeds to know what matters most in life. God bless both of them.

My sisters (Mrs. Anna Mrimi and Bahati) and brothers (Israel, Simon, Sunday and Baraka) also had their part in the success of this book. They have supported and motivated me not only through the entire process of my writing but also in every one of my endeavors. I want to thank them all including my father in-law, Mr. Bonphace Soka, and brothers and sisters in-law.

To the editors, Mr. J. Ulimwengu and Mrs. E. Holtz who did quite a good share of editing the book; and Mr. Warren D.M. Reed who did an excellent job finalizing the editing process before going to print. To the publishers, Mkuki na Nyota, I greatly acknowledge the wonderful contribution made to the success of this book; and especially Mr. Tapiwa Muchechemera, whose cooperation has been vital.

To all of those I have omitted, every person that has crossed my life's path; it was meant that we meet, either for a reason, for a season or for a lifetime. I learned something of value from each one of you. You may be pleased to know that I pass whatever good I learn down the generations as instructions. I take no moment for granted. I take no friendship lightly. I respect each and every one of you and with great love I say: thank you.

Foreword

Fifty years after independence, this book takes stock of how the economy has been managed under different leaders. It also evaluates ways to manage the consequences of colonization and the state of poverty of the majority of the Tanzanian people. The author recognizes the achievements of the different governments that have so far taken office in Tanzania, while giving an analysis of the different political frameworks and his view on how Tanzanians could realize their dream of the "Promised Land". It gives the perspective of what the author considers should be the policy focus, given the issues the country is facing.

Tanzania has emerged from a country that immediately after independence in 1961 recognized the need to focus on people centered development. While it is clear that over the years, different leaders have put different emphasis or weight on their policy objectives, the focus has never changed. The emphasis in the objectives of the different governments shows clearly that there was a careful consideration of not only the socio-economic state of the economy, but also the social, political and economic dynamics of the global economy.

This dynamism has propelled Tanzania through the tides of the global economy peacefully. The strong democratic process in Tanzania has helped to keep Tanzanians together, irrespective of their backgrounds or differences in opinion. This is no doubt, a major achievement, but not implying that there have been no costs to this cohesion. The social gains recorded in Tanzania came at an economic cost, which I would say, was necessary to build the foundation.

Tanzania embarked on broad-based economic reforms since the mid-1980s. The adjustment process under the reforms was gradual and at best cautious but steady, deep, and sustainable. This enabled Tanzania to achieve considerable macroeconomic stability, manifested by steadily declining inflation and gains in GDP growth. Inflation has been reduced from levels over 30 percent in the 1980s and early 1990s to single digit levels in the late 1990s and below 5 percent in June 2005. The fiscal imbalances of the past have been brought under control, while improvement in the investment climate has attracted both domestic as well as foreign investments. The Tanzanian people deserve much credit for these achievements.

However, despite the achievements, the challenges to the Tanzanian economy remain huge and downside risks, which could undermine the sustainability of these gains, are significant. Levels of poverty, particularly in rural areas, are still high and overall incomes are still low even by regional standards. This has been so, despite recent impressive growth levels. Domestic institutions remain weak and unable to translate recent economic achievements into real gains for the population. Similarly, while the expanding economy gives some ground for optimism, especially in terms of the ability of the country to finance its own development, Tanzania remains vastly donor dependent. The HIV/AIDS pandemic is having a devastating impact on the population, while global imbalances arising from recent high oil prices and increasing trade protectionism could slow down growth.

The author deserves much credit for clearly showing this dilemma, and articulating his views, in a very frank and honest manner. The initiative taken by the author shows not only his love and passion for his country, but also his lust for seeing a better Tanzania for everybody. I take this opportunity to congratulate him for the courage he has shown to venture in this difficult area and express his views so openly in this book. I believe that this book will act as an inspiration to all other Tanzanians who love their country, to come forward and air their views in a similar manner. As it has always been said, Tanzania *itajengwa na wenyewe*, and truly Tanzania will be built by Tanzanians themselves!

Dr. Joseph Leina Masawe,
Director
Economic and Research, Bank of Tanzania

Introduction

The late Julius Kambarage Nyerere was nicknamed "Musa" (Moses) during the later years after independence.

Although he was a fine politician and a philosopher, his nickname referred to a religious leader, Moses, in the early books of the Holy Bible.

It was, most probably, thought that there was similarity between Nyerere's role to Tanzanians and that of Moses to Israelites - delivering their peoples from slavery and leading them to a free land of prosperity – the Promised Land. Additionally, there was much similarity in the commitment with which these people implemented their visions. Similar to Moses, who was specifically directed by God to lead the Israelites, Nyerere regarded his role to lead Tanzanians as a divine responsibility and undertook it with great commitment and sacrifice. Like Moses, Nyerere died on the way; and thus like Moses, Nyerere never lived to see the fruits of the Promised Land.

Slightly similar to the forty-year Biblical pilgrimage of the Israelites, Tanzanians have their story chronicled in this book as also going to the Promised Land. After forty years, however, the Israelites reached the Promised Land. But after 50 years, the promised land is still too far for Tanzanians. It is such a contrast that brought about the title of this Book.

After 50 years: The Promised Land is Still Too Far! is a brief analysis of the political, economic, and social development of Tanzania since 1961. This analysis tells briefly about our fifty-year journey as a free nation: where we came from, where we are today, and most importantly, where we are headed. I, the author, discuss both sides of the contribution - success and failure - made by our three former presidents and their systems of administration: the late Mwalimu Julius K. Nyerere, Alhajj Ali H. Mwinyi, and Mr. Benjamin W. Mkapa. A review of both political and economic policies of our nation during this time is attempted, though I can, in no way, pretend to have covered everything that has happened in the specified time frame.

Much has happened during the past half century. Our political system has gone through a lot of changes: a year after our independence Tanganyika became a republic; just almost three years later, the United Republic of Tanzania was formed (in April 1964) after a successful union with the islands of Zanzibar. In 1967 the East African Community was formed; but collapsed in 1978. It is now under a careful reformation process with greater potential for success. Tanzania came from a multiparty system to unipartyism, and in 1992 back to multipartyism. We presently have several political parties–18 parties according to National Electoral Commission of Tanzania website. The book examines the contribution of the parties to the political development of this nation.

The economy has also undergone great changes during those years. The first administration, covering the period of 1960's, 70's and the first half of the 1980's, under Mwalimu, concentrated on agricultural economy with the ambition of strict adherence to socialism and with an almost "deaf ear" to foreign policies. During this time the first phase administration centralized almost all industries and Banks. Manufacturing of local goods in local industries were prioritized, and importation was done with a conservative approach.

The second phase (1985–'95) came with a different agenda to reverse the economic system to create a free-market with a more capitalistic approach. Importation of foreign goods was vastly allowed at this juncture of our nation's history. A conservative approach to build a sound economy was changed into a laissez-faire environment in which more room for economic dealings was created with less state intervention. The third phase (1995 – '05) embraced this approach. Privatization with hope for efficiency and more productivity was given high priority.

The social services: education, employment, and healthcare, which directly affect the lives of citizens, cover a great deal of discussion in this book. The effects of decentralization made by the second phase were felt everywhere, especially after the third phase implemented privatization with enormous rigidity. In the process many people, whose lives were fully dependent on employment in public organizations and the central government, were left unemployed after being declared redundant in a new, more efficient set up.

In fifty years more schools (from grade schools to universities) have been established; hospitals have been built. Private companies of different status are rampant.

However, we examine not only the number but also the quality of these services during the half century period. This is what constitutes the analysis of the past fifty years.

This analysis overlaps to the current phase and beyond. Our hopes and expectation on the incumbent president, H. E. Mr. Jakaya Mrisho Kikwete are also discussed.

After analyzing this journey, the goal has been to put forward suggestions concerning important areas of our country's economic development that require more attention, emphasis, and/or adjustments. In a nutshell, this book is about the past, present, and our progress to the future of our country economically and politically.

This book is not intended as a political campaign of any kind, for any party or any individual; however, I am trying to meet my intended goals, in the course of which I shall be forced to mention the names of some of our past and present leaders individually or collectively. I may also need to commend or criticize an idea, policy, system, style, move, belief, ideology or action. Be it known that this is with good intent. I do not mean to offend anyone down the road.

However, like most projects the preparation of this book has had setbacks. The difficulty in obtaining information and factual data has not only delayed publication but also lessened the scope of this book. Much needed information remained elusive during its preparation.

This book is expected to help the younger generation as a brief, yet comprehensive guide to the understanding of our nation's political and economic history. It may well be qualified as an instructive material for academic purposes and extra-curricular activities.

I am not a professional writer, and never have I been one before. So be ready for surprises. There was however, no better way to get my message across to you than by writing this book. I have decided, not because of higher intellect, but just like any other good Tanzanian, to share my views as a contribution to the common good, if any, of our nation.

It goes without saying that our country's history has taught us a great and valuable lesson. We have learned that "it's not what we have, but how we utilize it, that makes a difference." Therefore, employed here are facts that indicate how well or, sad to say, how poorly, we have utilized our natural, material, and human resources to get where we are today.

From Tanganyika to the United Republic of Tanzania

The United Republic of Tanzania is the outcome of a political merger of two individual states, initially known as Tanganyika and Zanzibar after their independence on December 9th, 1961, and December 10th, 1963 respectively.

These states were officially united on April 26th, 1964 after the Zanzibari Revolution of April 12th, under the strong influence of Presidents, the late Mwalimu Julius K. Nyerere (1922 - 1999) of Tanganyika and the late Sheikh Abeid A. Karume (1905 - 1972) of Zanzibar. The analysis in this book, while covering a greater portion of the merger, is more on the 50 years of Tanganyika's independence.

Administratively, Tanzania is divided into 28 regions, 23 of which are in Tanganyika (with two brand new regions). It has a total population of about 40 million people (2002 estimates) as compared to about 10 million people during the time of independence. As mentioned in the introduction, Tanzania has had four heads of state during the 50 years: J. K. Nyerere (1962 - 1985), A. H. Mwinyi (1985 - 1995), and B. W. Mkapa (1995 - 2005). H.E Jakaya Mrisho Kikwete is the fourth president of Tanzania (2005 -).

Tanzania is a republic. The President and members of Parliament are elected by votes in the general elections through democratic process every five years, with a limit of two terms to Presidents. The President has the mandate to appoint up to ten members to the Parliament. The President also appoints other high officials: the cabinet, including the Prime Minister (PM) and Attorney General (AG) and Ministerial Secretaries–Permanent Secretaries (PSs) Ambassadors to our diplomatic missions abroad; and other chief executives, e.g., Chief Justice (CJ), Chief of Defense Forces (CDF), Inspector General of Police (IGP), Director of Intelligence (DI), Director of Criminal Investigation (DCI), Governor of the Central Bank, Controller & Auditor General(CAG), Regional Commissioners (RCs), Regional Administrative Secretaries (RASs), District Commissioners (DCs), Court of Appeal and High Court Judges, Director Generals (DGs), Managing Directors (MDs), and Chief Executive Officers (CEOs) of different corporate organizations. The President also appoints and commissions many other committees for different short term, periodic and regular tasks and functions, e.g., the Electoral Commission, which will also be discussed in this book.

Up until 1977, when the permanent Constitution for the union was adopted, Tanzania used the interim Constitution of the United Republic of Tanganyika and Zanzibar of 1964, which was amended in 1965 and to which several amendments were made between 1965 and 1977.

For almost three decades the powers of the executive body were under the leadership of political parties – Tanganyika African National Union (TANU) in Tanganyika and Afro Shiraz Party in Zanzibar. On February 5th, 1977 these parties merged to form one party, Chama cha Mapinduzi (CCM), which continued to rule over the government. "The 1975 amendment (Act 8 of 1975), for instance, declared the supremacy of the party by providing that all functions of all the state organs were to be performed under the auspices of the party, a formalization of what had already happened." And in 1992 the 8th amendment paved a way for the multiparty political system.

Under the current Constitution, there is a provision under which the Zanzibari government operates, and for which it is responsible to the union government. This is to say then that there are two (one fully autonomous and the other semi-autonomous) governments within this union. Six Presidents have served as heads of the Zanzibari government: Sheikh Abeid A. Karume (1964 – till his assassination in 1972), Alhajj Aboud Jumbe (1972 – until his resignation in 1984), Alhajj Ali Hassan Mwinyi (1984 - 85), Idrisa Abdul Wakil (1985 - 90), Dr. Salmin Amour (1990 - 2000), Amani A. Karume, son of the first President of Zanzibar (2000 – 2010 and the incumbent Dr. Ali M. Shein (2010 - ?). Zanzibar is comprised of two small, beautiful islands (Pemba and Unguja) off the east coast of the country.

Dar es Salaam is the major commercial city of the country with a population of about 3.5 million (2002 estimates), and Dodoma is the legislative capital.

Tanzania is a multi-racial, multi-cultural, and multi-religious country with over 95% African-origin citizens. There are also citizens with Asian, European, and Arab origins. Kiswahili is the official national language and the medium of instruction in primary education. The English language is also used in higher level education and broadly in commerce and administration. There are over 120 tribes in the country, with the bigger tribes being Sukuma, Masai, Chagga, Haya, Gogo, Nyamwezi, etc.; but none of these tribes has a population of over a tenth of the country's population. Tanzania has two major religions: Christianity, which dominates in the mainland especially the west, north, south, and the lake zones; and Islam, dominating mainly on the east coast and the Zanzibar islands. There are also other religions like Buddhism, Hinduism, etc.

Tanzania is a member of many regional and international organizations and institutions: East African Community (EAC), Southern African

Development Community (SADC), once a member of Common Market for Eastern and Southern Africa (COMESA), African Union (AU), Commonwealth, and United Nations (UN). Throughout this book, the name Tanzania shall refer to this union of Tanganyika and Zanzibar.

While Tanzania is among very few nations in the world with a strong and stable social and political situation, her economy leaves a lot to be desired fifty years down the independence lane. Africa has experienced many changes of policies and/or leaderships through wars, strikes, protests, military coups or demonstrations in almost every state since the 1960s, but Tanzania was spared most of the time. Most of the political changes in policy and leadership in Tanzania occurred in a peaceful fashion. No major social or political upheavals have ever occurred in the country. No ethnic, racial, or religious discrimination has ever existed publicly in Tanzania. There have also been no serious cases of religious intolerance existing in the country. Peace has generally prevailed most of the half century.

However, there was minor religious and political chaos, e.g., an attempt to overthrow President Nyerere's government (1964), the Mwembechai demonstration protesting the capture of their fellow Muslims (February 1998), and the Zanzibar political standoff caused by dissatisfaction with the acts of the Electoral Commission (January 2001). Otherwise, Tanzania is said to be the only African post-colonial political federation that has survived. An initial attempt to unite neighboring Kenya and Uganda in the East African Community (EAC) was not very successful. A re-establishment plan to form East African Unity is in progress, and it is believed to have more potential to survive than it had earlier.

Unfortunately, on the economic side, we find a completely different story. The last fifty years have not been easy for most Tanzanians. The effort and commitment with which our leaders have served this nation have yet to bring what Tanzanians need and deserve. Very poor social services, poverty, unemployment, poor nutrition, disease, and corruption, etc., have been haunting Tanzanians throughout the 5 decades. We have heard many reasons being advanced to explain the decline of our economy, and we may wish to go through some of them briefly and see how much they did affect us and if they were controlled. In fact we need to. It is therefore very critical that we make a closer examination of these factors one by one and maybe suggest possible remedies.

1

The Country

Tanzania has everything that nature can bestow on its 343,317 square miles (858,292.5 km²) of land. Situated in the east coast of Africa, Tanzania is a beautiful and well-endowed country with abundant riches in terms of very fertile land, water sources from rivers and lakes as well as remarkable flora and fauna. Buried underground is a wealth of minerals. From its towering Mount Kilimanjaro – the highest mountain in Africa and the world's highest free-standing mountain, to the spectacular national parks of Serengeti, Ngorongoro, Manyara and Selous, teeming with wondrous species of wildlife, this is a strikingly beautiful country.

The Indian Ocean, which spans the eastern border of our country, is another natural resource that opens our country to the outside world, not to mention other marine activities notably fishing and recreation. Not only did God give Tanzania the Indian Ocean but also surrounded it with at least six neighboring countries without harbors, naturally leading them to become Tanzania's dependents when it comes to shipping and transporting cargo.

Fig 1: Mount Kilimanjaro

Mount Kilimanjaro, popularly known as "The Crown of Africa" or "The Roof of Africa," graces the skyline to the northern border; it stands at 19,650 feet above sea level. Hundreds of thousands of tourists from all over the world are attracted to this beautiful scenery, both to view and climb.

I would not like to tire you with long tales; neither would I want to sound like a nineteenth-century romantic poet, but just bear with me as we explore this beautiful land. You probably have never seen a parade of animals in your life. Do yourself the one little favor of traveling across miles of the magnificent land of the Serengeti National Park.

Popularly known the world over for the migration of animals, the Serengeti has up to two million animals on the march during the months of May and June every year as huge herds of wildebeest and other animals trek across the border into Kenya and back in search of grazing land. There are also other parks and game reserve like Ngorongoro crater, which is home to one of the world's largest craters and is a stunning site. The Olduvai Gorge has been termed the "Cradle of Mankind", and has been an important center for historic studies and a good attraction point for tourism.

We have hundreds of thousands of square miles of very fertile land for production of food and commercial crops. Tanzania also boasts great mineral resources, making it one of the richest depositories of minerals on the African continent: diamond, gold, tanzanite, copper, bronze, tin, aluminum, uranium, and many more. Natural gas is also found here.

Water in lakes, rivers and streams is everywhere in this beautiful country. Two of the world's important fresh-water lakes are also found in Tanzania: Lake Tanganyika, with about 250 species of fishes, and the second largest fresh water lake in the world, the largest in Africa – Lake Victoria – with various species of fish, some of which are not found anywhere else. Both of these lakes, serving as links to our neighboring countries: Uganda, Kenya, Democratic Republic of Congo (DRC), Zambia and Burundi are great natural resources.

The list could go on and on, but I do not want to make it sound like an idealized, fictional paradise. But probably the most important asset that Tanzanians can be proud of is that it has enjoyed unparalleled peace and tranquility at a time when other countries, both in Africa and across the World, have been rocked by war, civil strife and instability.

With such incredibly rich natural resources, I still cannot figure out why this well-endowed and beautiful country is so poor economically; there is no vocabulary that can capture the dimension of this paradox. This is why I am forced to agree with the paradox of the economists that, "all wealth comes from resources. Yet resource-rich countries are poor; and the resource-poor countries are wealthy." It is almost incomprehensible for such a country to be poor. With the amazing gift of all these resources, Tanzania is not only among the countries with least food exports but also her people suffer from hunger from time to time.

The abundant mineral wealth has not been exploited fully and has not been translated into any meaningful contribution to the nation's economy; consequently the economy has not been impacted positively; rather the tale has been one of occasional deaths of miners.

The waters flow everywhere in this country whose citizens have great shortage of clean water and insufficient electricity. The combination of all of these resources makes for the flow of tourists in the hundreds of thousands every year, and yet the value of our currency depreciates all the time.

With all these abundant resources naturally granted, Tanzanians remain among the poorest people across the globe, reduced to a class of beggars for foreign aid year in-year out. As a result we become a laughing stock to those who contributed largely to our problems. Sequel to all this is ineptitude evident in every sector of government, lack of foresight and apparent inertia, while human resources in the form of intellectuals have been leaving the country for foreign lands to look for greener pastures and a promising future, resulting in what is known as brain drain.

Currently, there is limited room for economic prosperity in Tanzania. This unfortunate situation can be ameliorated by undertaking radical and focused steps. The most important thing to begin with is to find out specifically where the problem lies. This will require comprehensive assessment of our current situation, how we got here and how we can get out of it. Many countries have turned their economies around, why not us? We need to learn from the emerging newly industrialized nations of South Asia, which are now considered among the world's fastest growing economies.

The problem must be diagnosed and a permanent solution sought. We need to analyze our economic situation clearly, make suggestions, and employ the most effective and innovative approach to solve the problems permanently.

Our leaders have tried to make sure that there is a better life for Tanzanians, but shortcomings either in policy or implementation have left a big gulf between the dream and the present reality. Some people are of the opinion that the mistakes might only have been human errors. Be it human errors or crimes, in the next few chapters of this book, I shall point out a few areas that need our enormous attention. I am going to refer to each of our presidents' regimes separately so as to evaluate each one of them and the contributions they have made towards the situation of the country as it stands today.

Economic Stance
"Tanzania is one of the poorest countries in the world." I have heard this phrase a million times; and I am sick and tired of it. In fact I am "allergic" to it. The thing that makes me feel worse is because it seems to be the most common opening statement of most reports and papers

about Tanzania's economy. I encounter it very often in newspapers, international economy reports, forums, websites, UN and IMF reports, International bodies, etc., and I think I have had enough of it. I need to hear something else, something better than that. I remember reading on a website once that "the position of Tanzania changed dramatically in the 1980s. It dropped from the 14th poorest country in 1982, with a GNP per capita of $280, to the second poorest in 1990, with a GNP per capita of $110." I exited that site immediately because I knew whoever wrote the information was not intending to write favorably of my country.

But somewhere, at the back of my mind, lies this fact of reality. My mind tells me that this is the truth whether I like it or not. It is the truth whether people say it or not. There is only one way to get rid of it; and that is to place our country among, the richest countries on the planet Earth. Something I am entirely convinced is possible. I do not want to put anyone into a fantasy world of daydreams but if others did it, why not us? It is now our turn. We need to get out of the sea of stereotypical thinking and work hard to rescue our nation by constructing a sound, flexible, and dynamic economy.

The Vision 2025 suggests something of hope, that by the year 2025 "Tanzania will have graduated from a least-developed country to a middle-income country." Graduations are good; and this one will probably be the most important graduation-to see Tanzania without the label of poverty. It probably sounds too good, but I know that it is possible sooner than later.

I hate poverty, and I am also convinced that there are many fellow Tanzanians with great hatred of the poverty that has turned out to be a stigma of our beautiful country. We have no choice but to make sacrifices for the progress of our nation and the future, better lives of our children and grandchildren. Most people I have had the chance to speak with feel that our political system needs a major overhaul in order to prepare a secure base and good grounds for the improvement of our economy. While I personally agree with the opinion, I also feel that there is much more to be done than just that. I shall not discuss it now, but it will make the latter chapters of my book worth reading.

Despite enjoying peace for decades, Tanzania, like many other countries, is not immune to socio-economic and socio-political problems. There is a good share of problems including poor social services, favoritism, a gap between the "haves" and the "have-nots", corruption, inflation, constant devaluation of our shilling, insecurity, unaccountability, lack of patriotism, theft, misuse of government funds, over-expenditure, high taxation, sexual harassment, abuse of human rights, diseases, and premature deaths.

These are some of the problems we have been wrestling with for the past 5 decades. What needs to be done in order for us to succeed in bringing this set of problems to a minimum should be a concern of every Tanzanian. We are brain-washed to believe that we cannot live without this mess. We think that these are necessary evils in our lives. This is incorrect! Tanzanians need to do something against this rampant situation. Our economic progress largely depends on our perceptions of our capability as a nation.

It is difficult to have definite answers to some questions with regard to our country's health of resources and her poverty; but what I have been made to understand from elsewhere is that it is solely a duty of all citizens both individually and collectively to see their country prospering. It is then a duty of every Tanzanian to contribute to the realization of our vision. For over fifty years now, since our independence, we have been blaming our leaders and each other for our failures and misfortunes. There is no time for that now; we need to change our viewpoint and realize that it is time to work, and it is time for each and every Tanzanian to assume a responsibility in building our nation, before which we should critique our policies and fix any wrongs.

Tanzania has had a number of development visions: the first vision, that of independence, was achieved successfully; the second vision came in February 1967, with the proclamation of the Arusha Declaration and the policy of Socialism and Self-Reliance, which was not a very successful experience; the third vision is contained in "Vision 2025", which seems to hold the promise of success; although it is still too early, we need to follow its course actively.

2

Former Presidents

No attempt is made in this book to criticize our presidents as individuals, but a few things are reviewed to measure the performance of their governments and the systems of administration under their leadership in order to help us understand where we are coming from and where we are headed. This will also help us point out to the current President what is expected of him.

In the last fifty years Tanzania has had four phases of leadership. These phases, here known as phase I, II III and IV, of our country's administration will be briefly but critically analyzed.

Phase I (1961 - 85)

Julius Kambarage Nyerere – The 1st President of Tanzania

As explained earlier in the introduction part of this book, the late Nyerere was once nicknamed Moses. This name likened Nyerere to the religious leader, Moses, in the early books of the Old Testament of the Holy Bible.

Nyerere had set himself the goal of delivering his poor nation from the yoke of colonialism and lead them to a future of prosperity, freedom and social justice. In this he assumed both political and social roles, and probably a spiritual role as well, just like the Biblical Moses before him. But like Moses, Nyerere died on the way; and like Moses who never made it to the Promised Land to see his people get milk and honey, Nyerere never made it to socialism where equality among the human race would prevail. Similar to Moses whose death occurred away from his people, Nyerere died away from his country while getting treatment in Great Britain; but unlike Moses whose body was never found to be seen by Israelites, Nyerere was brought back home and received the highest respect ever in the state funeral attended by about three million people from all over the world, making his the second biggest funeral in recent African history, following that of Gamal Abd-an-Nasir (Nasser) of Egypt in 1970. And like Moses, Nyerere was mourned for a month during which time every TV and Radio station aired songs about Nyerere, as well as his speeches.

As the Israelites crossed the desert, God used Moses to provide "manna" for them to eat as they were in transit to the Promised Land and could not produce food. Nyerere, during the transitional period provided Tanzanians with free education and free medical care for all. He also provided many other benefits like free housing and transportation to government employees. Although they both rose from very humble beginnings, the major portions of the lives of these great men were mainly spent in giving service to others, but both had very unanticipated endings.

Before his death, Nyerere had handed over official duties as president and remained as an advisor, a counselor, and a political problem-solver –the leader behind the scenes. The questions persist today: before and after Nyerere's death, is Tanzania still going to the Promised Land? If not, where are we going?

Over the years I have been made to wonder about the extent of this interesting comparison and who even thought of it. I find more to this prophetic match than just the similarity in the respective roles played by Nyerere and Moses. When I look at how we wander on our way like people lost in the desert, and how unpredictable our journey is, how we keep blaming our leaders like the Israelites did, and how older people recall those days of slavery as better days, I find a lot in common.

But sometimes I challenge myself with the fact that after forty years, the Israelites made it to the Promised Land; Tanzanians are still in an endless desert without much hope! After fifty years, more time than Israelites spent getting to their final destination, we are nowhere near the end of the journey. At least this is one significant difference between these two generations. In fact our Vision 2025 suggests that we still have over a decade before we arrive at another destination, and before getting to the land of promise. It seems as if it is going to take us a few more centuries before we make it, if we make it at all.

However, sometimes I look at it differently. I see a little difference in the estimated time of arrival to the Promised Land. In fact some of our fellow Tanzanians have already made it; or rather are enjoying the fruits of the land before they actually get there. These people are now enjoying the beauty and the prosperity of the land where some of us are having a difficult time figuring out if we actually are going to get there. While we are struggling day and night to survive, our fellow Tanzanians are enjoying the flow of milk and honey without regard to others. This is the second major difference between Moses' and Nyerere's generations. This land should have been a land of love and equality in fullness of time, but our compatriots were not so patient, and the rest have not been so lucky.

Nyerere was against the social classification of human beings. His dream was to see a society of pure equality and justice, especially when it comes to distribution of the wealth we make for ourselves. While I am not necessarily a proponent of this ideal, I am not an opponent either. I just respect the fact that at least Nyerere had a dream; he had a vision. This vision became the motivating factor of his entire struggle. It was the source of his political strength and the guiding principle of his career and the contribution he made to the welfare of his fellow Tanzanians.

In fact, one unique aspect that characterized Nyerere's administration was his courage to create new ideas and implement them for the welfare of his people. Nyerere did not have an imitation syndrome. He was courageous enough to pass through a pathway never tried before. He attempted new ways and ideas that were compatible with the standards of life of Tanzanians. His refusal to blindly copy capitalism or communism offers proof of this. He never wanted to become "a public relations officer" of the western world. In his administration, Tanzania chose to be non-aligned.

According to Dr. John Hatch in "Tanzania: a Profile", the non-alignment policy created criticism from both the West and the East. The West accused Nyerere of being a communist; and the East characterized Nyerere and his administration as liberal. But as Nyerere said, Tanzanians did not need a certificate of approval in its internal policies from any external group. The only approval of policy needed was the approval of the Tanzanian people. "The fact is that Nyerere was above all a humanitarian. He believed in human beings, regardless of their political or religious convictions," By John Hatch, wrote.

As indicated in earlier paragraphs, Nyerere's contribution started before Tanganyikan independence. He was among the freedom fighters that were determined to make Tanzania a free nation. His love for the country and respect for fellow human beings and his hatred for slavery and humiliation pushed him to great efforts into making sure that freedom was to be achieved. He achieved this goal. However, Nyerere's quest for freedom was not only for his country, but for the whole of the African continent. Therefore, he made major contributions to the freedom of many other African States.

After the first task of independence was over, Nyerere as the first President of Tanganyika and later of Tanzania, had the responsibility to change people's perceptions from the mentality of slavery to that of free citizenry, from working under colonialists' orders for the benefit of the colonialists to working willingly and diligently for the good of their own country.

It is clear that Dr. Nyerere understood exactly what was to be done; and he did very well at the beginning. He knew that he needed a prepared society and foresaw the danger that lay ahead if people were not prepared to accommodate freedom. Therefore, he started his leadership by preparing his people socially and psychologically. He built a very stable and peaceful society. He managed to make smooth social connections among people regardless of which end of the country they came from. He worked against tribalism and discrimination of any sort by words and deeds. It is evident that on this too, Nyerere did an excellent job, no doubt about it. At least this is one thing both the supporters and critics of Mwalimu Nyerere agree.

After the two primary tasks were accomplished successfully, Nyerere had yet to finish the job. He was in fact starting a very long journey: taking Tanzanians to a better country - a land of both political freedom and economic prosperity. After political independence the country's economic situation was of paramount importance. Herein lay a more challenging task for him, and perhaps also, left the stain on his leadership. Nyerere seemed to some people to fit so well into the English saying, "Great people make great mistakes."

Most people think that Nyerere was a great leader; yet many others think he was a big failure in terms of economy. His ideas on socialism seemed, to many, as a plan to build castles in the air. But to him socialism was not only attainable but also the ideal system for Tanzanians. He wanted people to cooperate in production and equally share the rewards of their labor.

Contrary to him, others felt that was too idealistic. Critics think that Nyerere missed a very important fact: that socialism is too sophisticated a system for a country like Tanzania, and was more so then. They think that Nyerere did not have an organized and sufficiently prepared team to achieve socialism. They claim that most of his people were still primitive and unlearned; most of them did not understand him, either.

On the other hand though, Nyerere believed that Tanzania would get to where he wanted it to go. He thought that in order for the people of Tanzania to be truly free they were first supposed to be fully self-reliant; and to him, the only right system was socialism. He opted for the African version of socialism (Ujamaa) that was compatible with the Tanzanians' lifestyle at the moment.

The late Nyerere - emphasizing a point during one of his speeches

Of course, he did not believe fully in the socialism from the former Soviet Union, especially some of the Marxist, Leninist philosophies like class struggle, authoritarianism, and Atheism, which were the lifeblood of the so-called scientific socialism (communism). He was strongly against the world's popular notion of taking Marxism and Leninism as religious prophecy to which every political opinion was referred for conformity. He emphasized his idea that socialism was secular; therefore nations should not be evaluated only by Marxism and Leninism ideologies as if they were religious prophecies.

History was not so much in favor of socialism though. The question was whether Tanzania would make it through this avenue. Be it possible or not, Nyerere had intended to realize his optimistic vision; but as one of his critics, Sven Rydenfelt, says in his essay on Lessons from Socialist Tanzania, "Good intentions are not enough. If you want to implement your vision, you have to start with a realistic blueprint." How realistic were Nyerere's blueprints for socialism, was not very clear then, and it is not any clearer now! There may have been a policy issue here and this may also be one problem inhibiting our economic development.

The economic situation in the 1970s and the 80s poses many difficult questions. The hardship of life that Tanzanians endured during these two decades was a bitter experience; it is in fact, as I mentioned earlier, partly the focus of this book. We have to know exactly what was wrong and why. Why was the Tanzanian economy deteriorating year after year? But the most important question is whether these mistakes were corrected after the good ten years of his successor, Alhajj A.H. Mwinyi, and the other ten years of the former president Benjamin Mkapa.

Records indicate that by 1961, Tanganyika was the greatest exporter of food crops in Africa, but by close to the end of Nyerere's reign (1983), Tanzania was ironically the greatest importer of the same. The cause of this deterioration may be partly attributed to the villagization program of 1974 and the nationalization of instruments of production, both being part of the implementation of the Arusha Declaration. After the government failed to persuade voluntary resettlement of peasants, even after promises of improved social services, it had no option left but the use of force, which aggravated the peasants who in turn decided to farm only enough for themselves - without surplus. This resulted in the great hunger of 1974 - 76 that marks Tanzania's lowest point of economy. This was another major mistake in this era.

Under socialist policies, instruments of production were to be state-owned and operated. So, a few years after independence, Mwalimu Nyerere placed all the major means of production under the government. This is technically said to be another error of this administration. Putting every industry (both manufacturing and service) under the government, which lacked competent manpower with sufficient managerial expertise to man the industries, was a sure way to destruction. Lack of proper management and supervision contributed greatly to a significant decrease in production and hence a drop in the country's exports leading to the weakening of the economy.

Investors and industrialists, especially "The Big Three" – National Bank, Grindlays Bank, and the Barclays Bank got a big surprise on February 6th, 1967. It was the day that the late Amir Jamal, then Minister for Finance, surprised them with the government's decision to nationalize all the banks and industries without any prior notice. It was announced to them that their power was ending at the close of business of the very same day. The government might have had a good intention, especially with the promise of reimbursing former owners, but its implementation marked the beginning of another major economic upheaval.

Trade disputes with Kenya also made matters worse. In pages 200 through 206 of translated "Uhuru na Ujamaa", Nyerere listed other factors and decisions in the 1960s and early 1970s that affected our economy, some seriously, some partially. These factors included: the boycott of

South African goods and the threat to leave the commonwealth if South Africa remained a member; the severance of diplomatic relations with Portugal over the country's colonial presence in a number of African countries; support for the liberation movement of Africa; the quarrel with and breaking off of diplomatic relations with the Federal Republic of Germany over the presence of an East German consulate in Zanzibar; disputes with USA; the disputes with the British government over Ian Smith's Unilateral Declaration of Independence (UDI) in Rhodesia; the establishment of diplomatic relations with communist China; non-alignment; ending of racial segregation in South Africa; and our commitment to African socialism

War with Idd Amin's Uganda in the late 1970s is also said to have contributed to our economic problems. In 1978, after Uganda invaded Tanzania and wanted to occupy some square miles of land in the Kagera region, Nyerere ordered our men and women in uniform to whip the late Idd Amin Dada – then the Ugandan president. Amin was punished severely and was driven out of Uganda when Tanzanian soldiers went as far as northern Uganda and captured the Ugandan capital (Kampala).

Apart from invasion, Nyerere's anger towards Amin was also due to Amin's brutality and dictatorship. Amin is said to have killed between 300,000 and 500,000 Ugandans during his dictatorship. Amin spent the rest of his life on earth in exile until death attended him in 2003. Unfortunately, his history was against him. Even his body was not to be accepted back in Uganda. He lived in exile, died in exile, and was buried in exile.

Incidentally, the Ugandan war did not turn out to be a success story economically. We won the war, but lost the economy. Almost thirty years since, we are still putting together the pieces of our nation's economy.

At times nature has also not been friendly. Many dry years have resulted in extremely low production in agriculture, which is the major source of our economy.

In the last few paragraphs above are the major contributing factors of the economic success and failure under the first phase.

However, Nyerere died as one of the most respected figures in the continent, and the world as a whole. His perfect combination of love for his fellow men, intellect, and integrity made him seem, at least to some people, like a saint. He loved his country very much. So much so that he sacrificed his own life for the country. Like his fellow great African leaders - Nelson Mandela, the late Nkwame Nkurumah, and the late Patrice Lumumba – Nyerere was popularly known and highly respected for his struggle against slavery, racial discrimination and humiliation.

Besides, Nyerere was also respected for his pure traditional African lifestyle. He was once described by an American official at United Nations as a "symbol of African hopes, African dignity, and African successes." (Chicken Bones – A journal)

Selfless, incorruptible, good-humored, visionary, and witty, Nyerere stood apart from many African heads of states. Nyerere was one of very few genuine advocates of unity, peace, and equality. He practiced what he preached. He was the author and implementer of the unity and peace that has prevailed for decades in Tanzania. He was given names like "Mwalim" (teacher) and "Baba wa Taifa" (Father of the Nation) because of his role in the nation. His intellectual and philosophical style of leadership made him a distinguished leader. Most Tanzanians liked him, except of course the few people who had an anti-Nyerere complex. His successors trusted his opinion and his vision for the country. It seemed as though no one could go to the Tanzania's highest office without consulting Nyerere and probably getting his blessings. Even some of the opposition leaders sought blessings from Nyerere in 1995, when we had the first multiparty election.

Julius Nyerere

When in power both successive presidents of the second and third phases evidently made frequent stops to Nyerere's home to fuel their leadership tanks. It was good to begin with him. Stanley Meisler, in his commentary paper "Saints and Presidents," of December 17th 1996 in Washington D.C, comments, "Tanzania was far better off with a benign saint for a president than a rapacious tyrant. I still admire Nyerere a great deal. But the Tanzanian experiment offers good evidence that saints do not really make very good presidents." Meisler may not have meant what he wrote, but in 2006, ten years of this statement and seven years after Nyerere's death, the Catholic Church in Tanzania was contemplating recognizing Nyerere as one of the saints. This will be the first time ever a politician becomes a saint and the first African to be recognized as such.

Nyerere received favor from each part of the world as a great leader. He was once described as "a president who is himself disciplined, self-sacrificing and dedicated, as well as honest and unpretentious, one of the rare 'philosopher-kings' (New Society, London). This man shall be remembered with such honor and great appreciation and his legacy will always remain.

Conclusively speaking, Nyerere did some good groundwork. Numerous changes were achieved in his era. His major accomplishments, among others, were: achievement of freedom; building a nation's identity; (this includes the union); creating peace and stability; fighting ignorance, disease, hunger and for equality of rights – there is still much to be done here. Nyerere accomplished some more notable achievements during the period of his leadership. One should never forget the man's significant contribution to the struggle for the freedom of other African states – South Africa, Namibia, Mozambique, Angola, Zimbabwe (Rhodesia), etc., that has built very good relations with these nations. Nyerere's name was known everywhere humanity was threatened. Even beyond the African continent, Nyerere was ready to stretch and support any human being who happened to be in difficulty. In the 1960s he strongly supported the civil rights movements in the USA. Among Nyerere's last roles was as chair of the reconciliation commission to Rwanda and Burundi. In 1997, Nyerere was elected as the chair of the seventy-seven poorest developing countries -G77.

On the other hand, many challenges also attended Nyerere's leadership. Some of these challenges persisted many years after he was out of office. Some of them were: unsuccessful implementation of the Arusha Declaration and the socialist agenda; continual decline of our economy due to many factors discussed here.

Reviewing Tanzanian political history, it is inadequate to make no mention of such people as Rashid Mfaume Kawawa. The late Kawawa was an integral part of the first phase administration. He was actually one of the architects of The United Republic of Tanzania, working hand in hand with the late Nyerere administratively, before and after union. Despite maintaining a very low profile as a leader, a very humble personality, and making a latent contribution, Kawawa has served our nation so honorably and honestly. He served in different capacities in the cabinet and public leadership. He has served as the second vice president of the union (1964 cabinet), Prime Minister (save Fredrick Sumaye, Kawawa was probably the longest serving Prime Minister in our country's history of 50 years) serving two times in this position (once prior to the union and later 1972 – 1977), Minister of National Service; Minister with Special Assignment and many other high government positions. Kawawa was a very close assistant to Mwalimu. Kawawa's loyalty was key to his successful service.

With the structure of the union, the Zanzibar President by virtue of his position was at times also the first vice president of the union. The late Abeid Karume was the first to hold this position followed by Alhajj Aboud Jumbe and all the other Zanzibar presidents until constitutional changes in 1995.

Again, omitting any mention of names like Edward Moringe, the late Sokoine (1938 – 1984) just seems atypical in the history of Tanzania. Sokoine served our nation with such commitment and zeal. He served as a Prime Minister, but of his own caliber. He also served two times, succeeding Rashid Kawawa from 1977 to 1980 and later in 1984. His strength of character and ethical standards were distinguished and brought as much hope to some people as they did challenges to others. He was a example of redemption to lower class Tanzanians. But doubts were everywhere of his being a match to the elite class or whether he was even accepted as much as he was in the lower class. Sokoine became very popular with his operation against "Uhujumu Uchumi" (Economic Sabotage) a few years before his untimely and mysterious death in a car crash at Morogoro on his way back to Dar es Salaam from a bunge (parliament) session in Dodoma in April 1984.

Like Nyerere the late Sokoine lived a sacrificial life. His down-to-earth character, modest lifestyle and high integrity explained it all. This was one Tanzanian political figure whose reputation was unmatched on the national level. There is no doubt that his death overshadowed Tanzanians' hopes and dreams. The end of his life was a strike to a Tanzanian dream. But his legacy will live on.

In the operation Uhujumu Uchumi of the early 1980s, Sokoine was determined to stop the economic sabotage done by people who hoarded commodities and sometimes even destroyed them in their efforts to cause scarcity and high demand and create what would look like the failure of socialism.

Alongside with this operation, Sokoine fought hard against Ulanguzi (black marketeering and unfair price hiking). He wanted to fight the economic iniquities of a few individuals who were bent on profiteering from the hardships that had been created by the deliberate scarcity of essential goods such as sugar, soap, rice, building materials (cement, roofing materials, etc.) and clothing. He wanted these goods and services to be available to more citizens than those few who accumulated them and eventually sold them for much higher prices. In a Tanzania which still harbored the ambition to build an egalitarian, socialist society, such activities were highly unacceptable crimes, and Sokoine went about eradicating them in the most emphatic, no-nonsense manner.

Sokoine was both popular to most Tanzanians and unpopular to few others with this operation. To a good extent, the late Sokoine succeeded in this operation but it was short lived. He died at the age and time that Tanzanians needed him the most.

Another great leader in Nyerere's cabinet was Salim Ahmed Salim. A diplomat by personality and by career, Dr. Salim was another close associate to Julius Nyerere administratively, especially in Tanzania's very successful international diplomacy. Dr. Salim spent much of his time in diplomacy in our embassies and international organizations. He has also served as Prime Minister, Deputy Prime Minister and Minister for Foreign affairs. At the international level, Salim served as the OUA Secretary and gained much prestige from everywhere in Africa and the world till his retirement in 2001, after an extended service of three terms (12 years) due to a record of good performance. He was also the first African and the first black person as a candidate for the post of Secretary General of the UN, strongly challenging incumbent Kurt Waldheim in 1980. His bid was thwarted only with an uncompromising US veto, and later Boutrous Ghali from Egypt became the first African and the sixth UN Secretary General, although Ghali lasted for only four years (1992 – 1996, this being the shortest duration a person has ever served as the UN Secretary General) before the second African, Kofi Annani from Ghana was elected in 1997.

Dr. Salim has also served many other cabinet, parliamentary, public and international positions including as president of the UN General Assembly 1979 and 1980. Dr. Salim is considered as one of the most renowned African diplomats with numerous recognitions, honorary degrees, and rewards in the areas of peace and diplomacy.

David Cleopa Msuya was another key figure of the first phase government. Serving twice a Prime Minister and First Vice President (1980 – 1983 and 1995 - in the second-phase government), and a couple of times as the Minister of Finance, Msuya has also served as the Minister of Trade and Industries. Keen, and a straight forward character, Msuya had good experience in national affairs. His competence made of him good presidential material and he ventured for the CCM candidacy in 1995; though he eventually lost to Benjamin Mkapa, who was finally elected president. Msuya was also one of the longest serving members of Parliament, representing Mwanga constituency for three decades. Msuya retired from public and political service in 2000.

Phase II (1985 - 95)

Ali Hassan Mwinyi – the 2nd President of Tanzania

Ali Hassan Mwinyi had been in the union cabinet for many years before his resignation for political reasons in 1974. However, he managed to survive and made his comeback in a big way when he became president of Zanzibar in 1984. Before his resignation, occasioned by his acknowledgement of vicarious responsibility for acts committed by his subordinates without his knowledge, Mwinyi had served in various union cabinet positions, including as minister for home affairs and minister for health.

In 1984 after Jumbe's resignation due to "polluted political atmosphere," Mwinyi was appointed as the acting President of Zanzibar and the Vice President of the union. He was later confirmed to hold the post. In the same year, Mwalim Nyerere announced that he would not run for presidency for another term in 1985. It is, until now, not clear whether Mwinyi was being prepared to hold office after Nyerere's term, but it is alleged that Nyerere had favored Salim as his successor, but pressure from some influential Zanzibari bigwigs did not allow him to have his way, and thus Mwinyi, quite unexpectedly for many, succeeded Nyerere as the President of the United Republic of Tanzania in October 1985.

Many middle and low income Tanzanians seem to commend Mwinyi's era over any other. The liberalization of trade and industry brought much relief to most people after the very conservative system of the first era. Many borders were re-opened for international trade and local internal business took a different turn. The first presidency had almost totally "turned its back to foreign ideas" and therefore there was little to accept from abroad. The second phase government, under Mwinyi completely changed this outlook.

Mwinyi's era is accredited with many development projects and major political changes. Among these was the rescue of industrial productivity in the early eighties. Between 1980 and 1984 our manufacturing sector was going down at an average annual rate of 5% - a negative growth rate. After the second phase came into power (1985) and adopted the Structural Adjustment Programs things changed. Our industries reported growth and between 1985 and 1989 there was a growth rate of more than 2.3%. This was a significant step from the negative growth that had been experienced.

It is unfortunate that supporting data of the second phase administration has remained by far the most elusive during the preparation of this book. But many projects were successful during this time; many donors offered to give aid during this period - perhaps because of the change of political ideology. Most major road rehabilitation and other important construction projects were agreed to in Mwinyi's time, though other projects initiated by him were actually implemented after he retired from office in 1995.

Rapid expansion of private secondary education is another notable change during the second phase of the government administration. Tanzania had highly restricted the expansion of private schools for decades prior to Mwinyi's leadership. But as both the population and the need for higher education grew, the government could not accommodate these changes with the limited resources of public education. This necessitated changes and in mid-1980 the government adopted new education policies, which prompted a rapid expansion of private schools and by 1995 Tanzania had registered 336 private secondary schools mainly financed by students' school fees. There were only 104 private schools when Mwinyi went into office.

Perhaps the most important political development attributed to the Mwinyi era was the smooth reintroduction of a multiparty dispensation. This transition from unipartyism back to multipartyism was quite a delicate process, and Tanzania is well commended for the way this change took place. While the super powers had to impose threats to force other countries like Kenya into multiparty policy, all Mr. Mwinyi had to do was establish a commission in 1991 for researching the opinions and views of Tanzanians to determine whether or not they were ready for the political and constitutional change. The commission under the then Chief Justice, the late Francis Nyalali, did an excellent job of collecting and analyzing those views. Ironically, most Tanzanians (over 80%) were still in favor of the single party system. However, the Nyalali's Commission, appending its report, advised Mwinyi's government to get into multipartyism. This was intune with the global political climate. The constitution was amended, and we stepped in multipartyism as peacefully as when we had been in unipartyism.

Another thing that seems a plus to Mwinyi's administration was to reduce the degree of power CCM exercised over national issues. CCM had grown to a point where it had accumulated almost unchecked status under the slogan, Party Supremacy - Chama kushika hatamu. Mwinyi's government rationalized the role and the powers of the ruling party.

Mwinyi is also commended for maintaining the peace and stability that he inherited from the first phase. His voluntary retirement was one example of this. Unlike many African leaders, Mwinyi followed Nyerere's style of contentment and retired willingly in 1995, becoming the first Tanzanian to fulfill the new constitutional law of serving a maximum of two terms as a president.

Finally, Mwinyi gained the love and respect of most ordinary-class Tanzanians. Most of these people thought that Mwinyi brought much relief into their lives; and up to this day he is still very popular among Tanzanians. (Among others, Mwinyi's achievements are: maintaining peace and stability in the country despite some minor chaos; Industrial Productivity growth rate; smooth transition to multipartism; more development projects started; and maintaining a small gap between the "haves" and "have-nots").

The satisfaction with which sections of Tanzanian society viewed Mwinyi's regime did not necessarily mean that the economy was growing, but at least people could choose what they wanted to do and do it, including moving away from Vijiji vya Ujamaa (Ujamaa Villages). There were fewer constraints during this era, but economists were not as happy as other people. They thought the country's economy was headed to the grave. What Mwinyi did was just a cosmetic repair to a much deeper problem. He wanted to solve the problems with just economic aspirin and band-aids in place of major operations.

Mwinyi was nicknamed "Ruksa" (permission) because of the laissez-faire style of his administration. Although still taking Nyerere's advice - as the ruling party's Chairman and as his predecessor, Mwinyi executed an about turn. He no longer wanted to pretend that he was practicing socialism. He realized somehow that socialism was not achievable; therefore, he moved smoothly from a socialist avenue of development to a more capitalist approach of economic improvement. This was partly the influence of the World Bank and IMF in the 1986 structural change agreement adjustments agreed with the Breton Woods institutions, with a view to correcting the macro-economic imbalances. Mwinyi never explicitly declared the failure of socialism, nor did he proclaim the genesis of capitalism, but implicitly the trend he set said it all.

At this point in time, liberalism was the only game in town. Economic, liberalism ruled. Stiff competition in search of, jobs, sales and markets existed among firms and individuals while the government watched and let the market decide. Mwinyi had indicated from the very beginning that he would immensely prioritize making a deal with the IMF. He allowed the private sector to take charge. Mr. Idd Simba, one of the country's successful politicians-businessmen and who has once a Minister for Trade and Industry in the third phase government who resigned after being accused of overstepping his authority to license importers of sugar, when being interviewed by BBC, said that "Tanzania had liberalised more than any other country in the region" adding "We were paying too high a price for our liberalising policy." He thought we had gone too far too soon on the road of liberalism and it was making us pay a high price. Simba's opinion, reflected a real situation that we were in at some point of our economy's journey.

Mwinyi's new policy opened up doors for foreign goods and importation, and businessmen imported goods like they never had before. Shops were full of foreign goods. Luxury cars were imported. Home furniture, garments, foods, and television sets flooded in the country. People were given more freedom to do whatever they wanted. Business, big and small, increased uncontrollably. Money circulation increased also, so it was easy for people to acquire and have a lot of it. Competition was left to determine our destiny, but iniquities of the economy were also part of the game. Some of these iniquities included: importation of expired goods, malpractice of professionals (incompetence in professional practices) and carriers (overweight in transportation, tax evasion, etc.), infringment of the rights and safety of laborers and workers, poor health care, increased environmental hazards, all these being fueled by corruption.

Everyone had a way, legal or illegal to make money. People saw no sense in hard work, and they became irresponsible. Workers reported to work and then left at will without having done any work and still got their salaries; production dropped and inflation went through the ceiling - up to 30%. Corruption was no longer fought against as much as before and so it increased tremendously. Soon we found ourselves on the edge of another extreme and our international reputation was seriously dented. At this juncture, corruption was a very common game. From the highest government official to the lowest employee, all danced the same tune. Social services got in very bad shape. The economy took a dive and Tanzanian life changed drastically.

This is also the period when a number of user fees were reinstated, i.e, school fees, medical fees, etc. But their re-introduction was couched in euphemistic soft-speak such as, kuchangia gharama za elimu, kuchangia gharama za matibabu (contributing to the health/education expenses).

However these fees did not reflect any relief on either side (the government nor the public) no betterment of social services as compared to the time when these services were provided free of charge.

During this era, government expenditures were also very high and misuse of government funds reached new heights.

One of the major political errors, however, that disgraced the second phase administration was the decision of the government to let Zanzibar into the Organization of Islamic Conference (OIC) secretly. In December 1992 Zanzibar subtly joined the OIC in violation of the country's constitution. Supposedly, the decision was made with the full knowledge of the deciders that it was against the Constitution of the United Republic. Claims were made that the decision was in favor of Zanzibar for reasons of economic benefit.

However, this was in complete violation of the rule of law as per our constitution. At this point, because of the unconstitutionality nature of the decision, Mwinyi faced a lot of pressure, from his predecessor, Nyerere, and the public at large, which went as far as demanding his resignation. Zanzibar was subsequently forced to withdraw from the OIC in February 1993, after a Parliamentary Commission ruled that this move was unconstitutional and as such unjustifiable. This was a disgrace to Mwinyi's administration as a whole.

On the social side, Mwinyi was also being accused of favoritism. This may not have been so obvious but it was claimed to exist in his system of administration. A comment on the Zanzibari Chronology website reads "Mwinyi has been accused of favoring Muslim and Zanzibari interests. He has repeatedly affirmed the secular nature of the state, but has done little to curb a growing fundamentalist attitude among some Tanzanian Muslims."

During his administration Mwinyi developed a practice of meeting with individual citizens who had problems - land problems especially, to get first hand information of their problems. Every week he would meet many Tanzanians at the CCM branch office at Lumumba Street. This practice, though meant to inform the President about the situation of corruption, did not last for long despite gaining popularity during that particular time. It was not feasible for the president of the country to attempt to meet every citizen with problems individually; in fact each citizen has at least one serious problem at any time in life and would cherish to meet with even a district officer, but he cannot. The President needs qualified assistants to help him solve problems.

Mwinyi's completion of his tenure in office was not a very pleasant experience politically, especially after the late Nyerere spoke publicly against the second phase weakness of excessive corruption terming it "wall-cracks" on a building. Mwalimu spoke critically about what he perceived as worsening corruption within Mwinyi's government. He resorted to calling Press conferences during which he would berate the government and its principal leaders for allowing corruption to become rampant, as well as for causing cracks to widen within the nation, thus undermining national solidarity and cohesion.

According to Nyerere, at no time was corruption as evident as in the latter years of the second phase government of our country's administration. Nyerere charged publicly that the country was "stinking" with corruption. It was not clear whether or not Nyerere's public declaration was politically motivated, or if there was a secret agenda. It is however, easier to suppose that Nyerere's behavior in those days was prompted by a genuine sense of moral outrage at the way business was transacted in government and the way corruption was becoming accepted as the social norm rather than a legal offense; therefore, he felt the need do just that.

Nyerere was also heard bitterly reprimanding those whom he thought entertained ideas with signs of destabilizing the union. He especially targeted the Prime Minister, John Malecela and the CCM General Secretary, the late Horace Kolimba. According to Nyerere these were the "guys" who had misled President Mwinyi on this issue and because Nyerere had never taken kindly any threat to the stability of the union he became furious.

Among the prominent people who served under Mwinyi in the second phase government, apart from Malecela, mentioned above, we note the contribution of Judge Joseph Sinde Warioba, who served as Prime Minister and First Vice President between 1985 and 1990. He was succeeded by Malecela, who served between 1990 till 1994, when Nyerere pressured Mwinyi to replace him, and for a brief period between 1994 and 1995 Cleopa Msuya was the Prime Minister.

Msuya then retired, but Malecela remained Vice Chairman of the ruling CCM party till after second and third phases. Mr. Yusuph Mkamba was later added to strengthen CCM party's top three.

Malecela also attempted to secure his party's nomination as a presidential candidate in both 1995 and 2005. In 1995 for whatever reason, after a very intensive preparation, very improbably Malecela removed his name at the very last minute. Again, rumors went around from Dodoma that Nyerere enormously influenced Malecela's decision! Malecela's second attempt in 2005 came to naught as he was thwarted by his boss, Mkapa, even before the elimination process had started.

A lawyer by profession, Judge Warioba served also in other positions namely State Attorney, Attorney General and Minister for Justice, Minister of Works, and a judge of the International Tribunal for the Law of the Sea, plus many other international positions and delegations. Nonetheless, something mysterious seemed to surround Judge Warioba's political career. He was among the people most likely to become President in the second or third phases. Most Tanzanians were actually in favor of Warioba as a more capable candidate and his name kept lingering in people's minds, but it was either the system or lack of quest on his side that kept him away from Presidency. In 2003 he became the President of the UDSM Convocation.

Judge Warioba is now semi-retired, and is currently working as a private advocate, although he continues to consult with the Government on matters of corruption.

One of the most colorful episodes of the Mwinyi's era has to be the appointment of a radical politician, Augustine Lyatonga Mrema, first as minister for Home Affairs and later as Deputy Prime Minister and Minister of Home Affairs. It was during this time when the position of Deputy Prime Minister was re-established unconstitutionally and Mrema who was presumably doing a good job in the Ministry of Home Affairs held the post. A general viewpoint was that this position was established to reward Mrema and expand his territory of power.

Mrema was said to be a very hard worker with on-the-spot solutions to many social problems. He also briefly became very popular to most ordinary Tanzanians. However, his overzealous approach to his duties put the odds against him. He eventually outdid himself when he grew an appetite for attacking his own government while still a minister. He got the inevitable sack and found himself in the opposition, challenging very strongly for the presidency in 1995. However, he lost to Mkapa, and since then his earlier popularity has faded, and he has now practically dropped off the political radar screen, but his faith keeps him going. He now remains an MP from Vunjo and keeps supporting CCM on almost every agenda. Paradoxicallt, Mrema opposed CCM when he was supposed to support it; and now he supports CCM from the opposition side, when he's supposed to oppose it.

Phase III (1995 - 2005)

Benjamin William Mkapa – The 3rd President of Tanzania

In the 34th year after the independence of Tanganyika, Benjamin William Mkapa stepped-in as the third president of our nation. Mkapa emerged like a tiny flower in a huge forest. He had been working for the government in high and public positions since the 1980s, and had been in the Cabinet for two decades prior to his nomination as a CCM presidential candidate, but Mkapa was not very popularly known by most ordinary Tanzanians as compared to some of his fellow candidates and opponents. It is, perhaps, due to the fact that for quite some time he served outside the country, as High Commissioner and Ambassador to Nigeria, the USA and Canada.

Mr. B. W. Mkapa was initially Nyerere's personal choice, and later seemed to gain approval from almost every CCM member and eventually the entire Tanzanian community. He had gained more approval from the late Nyerere who was once his teacher, because of his conduct. It was alleged that Mkapa became CCM's and Nyerere's candidate after Nyerere's efforts to have Salim Ahmed Salim present himself for the presidency failed because Salim would not leave his post as Secretary General of the Organization of African Unity in Addis Ababa. This was the second time Nyerere had tried to make Salim president, after his earlier attempt in 1985.

After Salim declined Nyerere turned to Mkapa and after a grueling campaign against a vibrant and crowd-pulling Mrema, Mkapa was elected president. A lot in Mkapa's victory owed much to Nyerere's personal efforts put into the campaign, moving from rally to rally carrying Mkapa's posters urging the country to "vote wisely" for the good of the nation. However this support was overshadowing Mkapa's credentials as a competent candidate as people were bound to see him as a candidate imposed by the immense prestige and influence of Nyerere.

Nyerere did more than just promote Mkapa in 1995. He also jeopardized the opportunity for Edward Lowassa who was probably the most likeable and most admired presidential candidate of that time. Nyerere did what is termed as character assassination to Lowassa who would probably become the greatest challenger within CCM after John Malecela removed his name at a very early stage. The Tanzanian public did not seem to agree with Nyerere's opinion at that time, but once again Nyerere got away with it subtly. Then, Mr. Lowassa understandably kept a very low profile, which might be the hard way but the only way for an upcoming politician like him.

Mr. Mkapa was prompted with the nickname, "Mr. Clean." This implied that his work records and files from the Intelligence Department suggested no history of misconduct whatsoever, which increased optimism among many people. In a country so saturated with corruption, this kind of label could serve a politician a good deal, and this was true in the case of Mr. Mkapa. Nyerere emphasized this aspect of Mkapa's personality, and because Tanzanians knew Nyerere to be genuinely an upright man, they did as he told them to.

Mr. Mkapa entered the office with some advantage. He was like a reserve player of a soccer team who had been watching and following the game all along. He knew not only the mistakes of his teammates but also the weaknesses of the rivals. He had observed two extreme points of the country's political and economic systems, in which case he was a part. Therefore chances were good that he would regulate the system and do better.

All the same Mkapa had to face a challenge that the two men who went before him, Nyerere and Mwinyi had not had to face. Multiparty politics, which had been practiced for a very short period after independence, had been re-introduced just three years before the general elections of 1995. Since 1965, the one-party system had meant that the official candidates at presidential level were practically unbeatable since they were running against themselves, really, with the electorate to mark "YES" or "NO" on a piece of paper that had only one name and picture for the "YES" and a blank with no name for the "NO".

Mkapa was going to have to face real opposition and tough challenges, not only in the elections but also during his leadership. He had a number of opposing candidates running against him and against each other. The challenge that Mkapa got from his competitors was real, but with the energetic campaigning of Nyerere, he won. Augustine Lyatonga Mrema of the National Convention for Construction and Reform (NCCR – Mageuzi), who had just gotten out of CCM about seven months earlier due to disagreement with his party policies and who had risen very fast to high level positions, and Prof. Ibrahim Lipumba of Civic United Front (CUF), were Mkapa's biggest challengers.

Mrema was, according to polls by local papers, more popular than Mkapa, who won the election with a comfortable majority anyway. He got 61.8% of all votes against NCCR's Mrema, who got 27.8% and the CUF's economics professor, Lipumba who got 6.4%. These giants left some 4% of the votes for the less popular, but famous and confident candidate, John M. Cheyo (Mapesa) of the United Democratic Party (UDP). CCM took 186 seats among the 232. NCCR had 24 seats and the remaining were from CUF.

After he won the general multiparty election, Mkapa was then facing the real deal. From the outset his government seemed to put emphasis on the decentralization of most public responsibilities to local governments and private sectors and chose to concentrate on governance and a few core responsibilities. This was meant to enhance performance and efficiency, which were evidently the crowning virtues of the third phase government.

Mkapa entered the state house with modesty. He did not want too much attention. He asked the media not to put his name in the front page of every newspaper. He refused to be on the currencies. Even during his presidency, he did not want to name things, like streets, buildings, etc. With his name, something that had happened before him.

Mkapa also indicated right from the start that he was concerned with the levels of corruption in the country. He had worked in government for many years and knew corruption by the real meaning of the word. Therefore, he wanted to get rid of corruption or at least reduce it to a minimum. He promised his voters, and those who voted against him, that he would do whatever it would take to fight the battle against corruption. He established new organizations and agencies to lead the war.

The Prevention of Corruption Bureau (PCB) was a brand new name given to the already existing corruption institution (Anti-Corruption Squad) that was specifically for the corruption war, but this time with a different strategy. With the aid of the police force new strategies and policies were put in place to combat corruption. It was during this time when the so-called police money was circulated and people were arrested, and others lost their jobs and respect because of the traps of the corruption money.

Mkapa also established the cabinet position of Minister of State for Good Governance in the President's office, charged with, among other responsibilities, the fight against corruption.

To demonstrate his seriousness in this fight Mkapa appointed a presidential commission to look into the various facets of corruption in the country and propose to him ways and means to curb the plague. Judge Joseph S. Warioba, the former Prime Minister, was appointed the Commission Chair, and after several months of arduous work the Commission presented its findings to the president, who made them public and promised to work on the recommendations.

Another problem that Mkapa wanted to get rid of was the government's debt (international and local). This is one area in which the third phase did an excellent job. Debts were serviced sufficiently well for Tanzania to qualify for a huge relief from international donors under the enhanced framework of the Heavily Indebted Poor Countries (HIPC) initiative.

In 1997 Tanzania had a total external debt of about US $ 7.8 billion. In 2001 Tanzania became the fourth beneficiary (after Mozambique, Bolivia and Uganda) to be exempted a total of US $3 billion as debt relief. The money that should have gone into paying these debts was thus freed for investment in the social service sector. Primary school pupils were enjoying education paid by government funds as a result of the debt relief to Tanzania. According to the IMF report this relief came as a result of "continued progress in implementing sound macroeconomic and structural policies and the overall quality of its Poverty Reduction Strategy Paper" by the third phase government.

Mkapa was apparently very much against improper tax collection and mismanagement of government funds. He came up with new structure and strategies for better tax collection. The Tanzania Revenue Authority (TRA) of July 1996 was established purposely to improve tax administration. "Prior to June, 1996, tax administration was under independent revenue departments, which were operated within the civil service framework under the Ministry for Finance, which was responsible for the direction and control of the departments." (www.tra.go.tz). But the malfunction of these central government entities made Mkapa to seek an alternative scheme to improve revenue collection. One sure way was through an improved tax administration system, thus TRA was founded in 1996.

Mr. Benjamin Mkapa

He was determined to boost government revenues and capital formation strategy for investments. No doubt about it – he managed to do so. Taxes were collected. And by the end of the first financial year after establishment of TRA, the government revenues were clearly high, much higher than the year before, and continued on that trend. In the financial year 1996 - 1997, the total collections were 267.1 billion. This marked an increase of 36% as compared to the previous year's total collections of 196.5 billion. The highest increase was recorded in the following year when a total of about 491.1 billion, an increase of almost 84%, was collected. In 2010/2011 TRA estimated an average monthly collection of 430 billion as compared to 25 billion before TRA. This is an increase from the average monthly collection of 85.5 billion in the financial year 2002 – 2003. The total collection of 2003 - 2004 stood at 1.459 trillion. In the 2010/11 financial year it was 5.25 trillion, an increase of 18% from the previous collections. This is, evidently, another significant improvement.

Nevertheless, TRA were the happiest on Dec 2011 by having a record monthly collection of a staggering TZS. 685.5 billion and surpassed their target by TZS. 40 billion. According to the Acting Director of Taxpayer's Service and Education, this was the first time TRA had gone so much higher than their target. The major attribute of this record collection was, of course, the introduction of Electronic Fiscal Device (EFD), an electronic device that was made mandatory to all Valued-Added Taxpayers (VAT) registered clients. According to the report by November 2011, 92.3% of all VAT registered businesses countrywide had purchased the EFD. Another attribute to this growth was said to be the awareness campaign on the importance of paying taxes.

Below is the chart representation of the total annual revenue collections during the last 5 years (TRA).

Table 1: Revenue Collection

Yr	95/96	96/97	97/98	98/99	99/100	00/01	01/02	02/03	03/04
Tzs (Bil)	196.5	267.1	491.1	548.0	662.0	770.2	918.3	1119	1459

The chart below represents a good job done by the third phase government in improving revenue collections through different taxes and fees.

Ministry of Finance has, nonetheless, been highly accused of dubious tax exemptions. Ministers have engaged in exempting taxes where there is no economic advantage to the nation. In 2010 for instance, TRA was said to have lost 680 Billion shillings through exemptions. Yet, this was 10% less than 2009 exemptions. Source: http://www.hakielimu.org

Mr. Mkapa also tried quite successfully to control inflation, which by then was exceedingly high. He was determined to drop it to a one digit percentage. Just three years after he assumed power, inflation dropped from 30% to as low as 13%. Using the Central Bank and other financial institutions, money circulation was controlled and soon the outcome was obvious and the goal was met – one digit inflation percentage was achieved by the year 2000. The inflation rate by 2004 was 4.7% - the lowest rate our country had ever reached since the late 1950's.

Fig. 2: Total Revenue Collections 2006 - 2010 and 2011 Projection

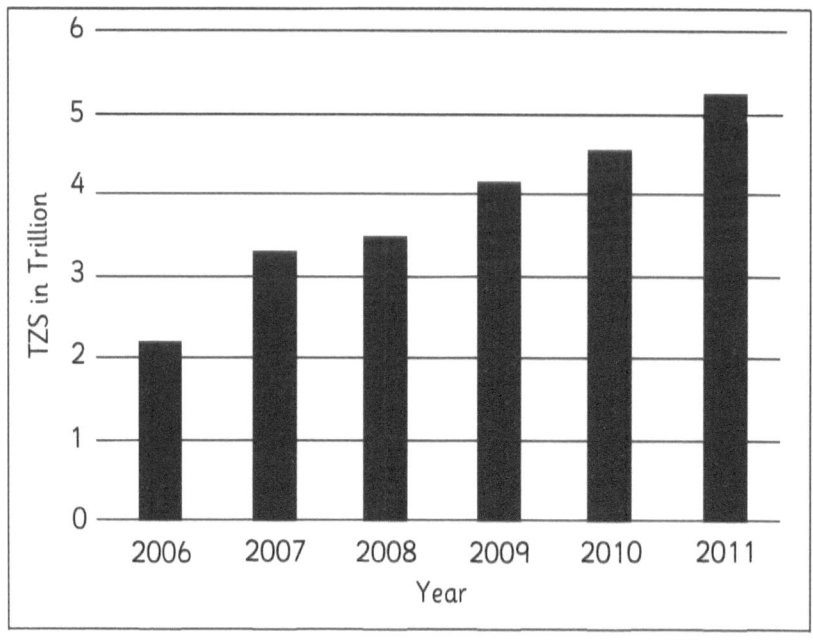

Source: URT

Lack of discipline at work was another major problem and a great hindrance to economic growth. Mkapa wanted to rebuild work discipline and proper management. He made a lot of changes in the system trying to come up with the best system.

Mkapa was also a good 'Construction Engineer'. There has obviously been good progress of performance on road rehabilitation and construction. Many projects have been accomplished in the second and third phases. Some of these completed projects include 68 km of roads expansion projects; construction of macadam roads of about 200 km; construction of Mkapa Bridge and 22 other bridges; possession of Kilombero and Ukara crossings; and many others. Ongoing projects include construction of a total of 961 km of macadam roads; rehabilitation of more than 197 km of roads; and other major and minor projects. Whether this was enough input for the ten year period is a question to be discussed.

The Third phase government's attention to the concerns of teachers' and soldiers' salaries is another success attributed to Mkapa. Teachers and soldiers had suffered neglect in terms of delayed and insufficient income for so long. Teachers especially, would work for months without receiving even the little salaries they rightly deserved. Mkapa determined to follow up these issues and appointed a commission to investigate the chronic problems that surrounded this important section of any country's development. This is probably among the very few commissions in the history of our country whose recommendations were actually changed into action by the government. Although not all problems were resolved, today teachers and soldiers perceive Mkapa as their redeemer.

Cleanliness in Dar es Salaam is commendable. It is reasonable to credit people like Charles Keenja and Lieutenant (rtd) Yusuph Makamba (former City Commissioner Chair and the former Dar es Salaam Regional Commissioner, respectively) for their efforts in changing Dar es Salaam into a better looking, cleaner city. They both made a significant contribution towards the improvement of Dar es Salaam, which for many years looked like a dumpster when compared to cities of neighboring countries.

On the other hand, Mkapa used his presidency quite advantageously. He might have started with a low note, but it is obvious that he finished with a very high note, in contrast to his predecessors, both of whom did not finish as well as Mkapa did. Not many people thought Mkapa would be as successful in such a torn apart economy. But after ten years, Mkapa managed to restore Tanzanian reputation outside, and gained for himself an international recognition as yet one of the most successful leaders of the new era Africa who managed to expose the country to international trade and investment. Most foreign countries seem to appreciate his governance and he has been given international responsibilities because of his performance. He was, for instance, appointed, together with the President of Finland, in January 2002, to co-chair the World Commission on the Social Dimension of Globalization and in 2004 he was again appointed along with 9 other African leaders to form Tony Blair's 19-member commission for Africa.

Having analyzed the positive side of the third phase administration, discussion of the dark side of it is inescapable. The following are the political and economic areas in which Mkapa's government failed to meet Tanzanians expectation. Disappointingly, Mkapa made very strong promises in some areas, and in each one of them, his government failed to offer results.

A few years after Mkapa finished his term in office he was haunted by the consequences of his dealings while he was still in power. The next administration, in an effort to make right what was wrong found itself stumbling upon stunning revelations on a sealed chapter of history that was never meant for everyone to read. These revelations introduced, in true colors, the former Head of State, formerly nicknamed, *"Mr. Clean"* to his fellow Tanzanians. These revelations also gave a true picture of what was behind the scenes of Mkapa's leadership and whether or not the current administration was capable of taking this nation to the next chapter. Mkapa's administration seemed to have been connected to numerous dubious contracts as well as bogus registered companies. Companies like Kiwira, which engaged in Coal Mining and Electrical Power production in Mbeya; Meremeta LTD, a gold Mine company that did its mining operations in Buhemba, Mara Region from 2003 to 2006 when the company declared bankruptcy; Tangold which was said to have had taken over from Meremeta LTD in 2006; and others, which were accused of misconduct and corruption and were linked with the former President and his close associates. However, no legal actions were taken on the allegations leveled against these companies or Mr. Mkapa himself.

Many mistakes prevailed in both general elections during the third phase, some of these were just minor, but some were monumental, such as open corruption in the process; misrepresentation of information in reporting; rigging of votes; threats and even physical beatings by the police. Not only did Mkapa fail to better the situation, but he also convinced himself that the elections were free and fair. He was probably the only one (apart from his assistants) who developed such an opinion despite the obvious shortcomings. But Tanzania should be governed by principles and laws and not opinions. Due to that failure people lost trust with the Electoral Commissions in both parts of the union.

Despite Mkapa's early promise to deal with the problem of corruption resolutely, it is clear that a lot was not done. With the newly named PCB, currently PCCB, Tanzanians had hoped to see changes in the short term, but soon rumors spread all over that PCB was like a doctor who acquired the disease for which she was treating the patient and both became patients without a doctor. The idea to have PCB is no doubt worthwhile, taking into consideration the level of corruption Tanzania had reached. However, the PCB needs continuous reshaping and remodeling to make it function as a reliable, strong, incorruptible, and independent organ.

The third phase administration started the war against corruption with something of a barking dog stance. After a period of a lot of barking, people believed the dog in the neighborhood would probably counter inappropriate activities. Likewise, the barking style gave some credibility to the third phase government, especially among the donor community because it sounded like corruption was being dealt with. But in reality it was not. What Mkapa's administration succeeded in doing, however, was to create an atmosphere of trust inside and outside the country that corruption would be done away with. The advantage on the side of the government was the complexity of corruption and the guaranteed secrecy of the environment in which corruption takes place. At least, by talking against it, the Mkapa administration got credit.

Corruption is a very dangerous ill but it has just been made a thing of politics. It has actually been institutionalized and formalized and has been given pseudonyms and euphemisms like Kitu kidogo (Just something little), Takrima (appreciation), lunch, soda, Ahsante (thanks), nauli (fare), voucher, etc., depending on its magnitude and the demand. In the same cause there are so many issues about corruption that are pending – with no government explanation. The formation of the PCB and the Warioba Commission just added a chapter to the history of Tanzanian corruption.

A reference is made to the conference paper on "An Overview of Benjamin Mkapa's First Five Years" by the Department of Politics and Public Administration at UDSM and is quoted here as follows:

> *However, for many living in Tanzania, it is difficult to square the perceptions of reduced corruption with the reality of dealing with state officials. In this paper we argue that while the Mkapa government has been able to restore outside trust in the government, it has been less effective in reducing the day-to-day corruption that has come to characterize the average citizen's dealings with state. The Mkapa government has not taken a pragmatic approach to curbing corruption. That is, aside from rhetorical condemnations, there has been a marked absence of commitment on the part of top leaders to change the system or to empower the public so that they can hold accountable those with positions of authority.*

The so-called Warioba Report received a number of plaudits within Tanzania and abroad, but soon there was skepticism as to whether its proposals were being taken seriously by the government.

Mismanagement of funds was and still is a problem. Between 1999 and 2001 for instance, there were reports of 125.4 billion improperly accounted for. This is still a big problem to date.

The third phase government failed to put into practice their slogan of transparency and truth. There were so many issues that were never clear to Tanzanians during this phase, especially about corruption and other misconducts in governance.

Making Dodoma the capital city is another recorded failure. And it is only a failure because it was so used to making promises during Mkapa's campaigns.

This is not significant, but it is worth mentioning. The third phase administration, like the first and second governments, failed miserably on this too. The only question is why every president thinks this is an idea to impress people. Nyerere wanted the government to move to Dodoma, but it never did. Mwinyi supported the move, but never accomplished it. Mkapa came in with even stronger determination – he also failed. I must admit I am quite ignorant of the pros and cons of making Dodoma a capital. The specious argument that it is centrally placed and secure for terror or attacks is immaterial in an era with long range missiles. The question now remains: why should presidents and candidates make it a political agenda in every phase? Mkapa seemed the most determined President to move the nation's capital from Dar es Salaam to Dodoma; but that remained rhetoric.

The cabinet size was another issue that took much weight in Mkapa's campaigns. Mkapa made strong promises to reduce the size of the cabinet, but ended up doing exactly what he promised not to do. The Cabinet kept increasing. By 2004 there were 19 full ministers for independent ministries. 4 ministers were in the President's office, 2 in the VP office, and 2 in the PM's office, plus the Attorney General and 16 deputy ministers and Permanent Secretaries. This does not seem to be a small cabinet for the size and population of our country then. And the repeated promise of new faces in the cabinet just proved Mkapa wrong.

Economically, the third phase government also disappointed Tanzanians. In very simple terms the only practical economic improvement would be a better life. But Tanzanians cry out loudly in their demand for a better life. This still remained a dream, wishful thinking – an unfulfilled desire throughout Mkapa's administration. The third phase government completely failed to bring practical changes in people's lives. The claim of economic growth versus the increasing hardship of life was a mystery. It is an unresolved puzzle for the current administration, and to my opinion, this is where the current phase government should concentrate its efforts. It is so sad to say that the last administration has done tremendously well in some areas, but performed very poorly in other more important areas. There was no consistency in performance.

Judge Joseph Sinde Warioba, in his opening remarks on the occasion of 2003 University of Dar es salaam Convocation Symposium commented "Because of the reforms, there has been significant economic and social improvement....This significant achievement has not however reduced poverty. Abject poverty has in fact increased, particularly in the rural areas."

President Mkapa took special pride in making surprises of the nomination of his assistants. After surprising Tanzanians with his choice of the Prime Minister at the beginning of his leadership by picking low-rated Frederick Sumaye, he also came up with an unknown scientist as his VP – Dr. Mohammed Ali Shein. However, unlike Sumaye, Dr. Shein brought with him a wealth of expertise and experience in both professional and political matters. He served as the Vice President for the third phase. Dr. Shein's political career goes as far back as the late sixties when he was a leader of the Afro Shiraz Party Youth League (ASPYL); but he was almost totally unknown in the mainland. Not until 2001, when he replaced another likeable Tanzanian leader, the late Dr. Omar Ali Juma, was Shein known to the general public.

Dr. Ali M. Shein, Vice President (2001 –2010)

Dr. Omari A. Juma was the Vice President from the beginning of the third phase. His untimely death was a big blow not only to the third phase government but also the nation as a whole. This was the third time death had attended the top executives of government in our country while still in power. Karume and Sokoine had also died as heroes in the line of duty.

Dr. Shein came back again as the fourth phase vice president under the Kikwete's administration. In 2010 he become President of Zanzibar.

Mkapa chose to have one and only one Prime Minister throughout his entire presidency. There is of course, nothing constitutional against his preference, but many people did not and have not understood the secrecy behind this inflexibility in the choice and maintenance of Sumaye as the Prime Minister. Nevertheless, this was another aspect that characterized Mkapa's administration – he did not make frequent changes in his cabinet as did the earlier governments under Nyerere and Mwinyi. Even when rumors and allegations of misconduct went around, he was either very prudent or slow to act. Therefore there were many other ministers who also stayed in the same ministries throughout Mkapa's presidency.

Sumaye was a real surprise to Tanzanians from the beginning. With very ordinary credentials and no international reputation whatsoever, Sumaye very privileged to hold the position of PM at that eventful time of the country's history. His political career began just eight years prior to his nomination as Prime Minister. He had served for seven years (1987 – 1994) as Deputy Minister for Agriculture and a year as the Minister in the same Ministry, and after that he became the PM.

Apart from being the seventh Prime Minister in Tanzanian history and despite being the longest serving PM, Frederick Sumaye's account does not contain any outstanding record of performance. Unfortunately, he was also haunted by rumors of corruption from time to time, which formed a cloud of doubts around him in the minds of many Tanzanians. However, Sumaye still held strongly to the belief that he was good and even fit for Tanzanian presidency. He had the courage to contest for the CCM presidential candidacy just to end up realizing that appointments are different from election by votes based on competition, competence and political popularity. He did not reach the final.

After a general review of all the three phases, it is important to see where we stand economically by taking stock of our political, economic and socio-economic success and problems. And because we cannot mention each one of them in the few pages of this book, I am just going to select a few areas and attempt to make a partial scrutiny of our position.

3

Social Services

Health

The Ministry of Health is responsible for health administration and all health-related issues. Many changes have been recorded in this sector since 1961. Like other sectors, the health sector has made significant improvement in administrative matters and in growth in terms of numbers. This improvement includes increases in the number of health facilities and personnel, changes of policy, establishment of numerous institutions, policies, etc. The Muhimbili National Hospital (MNH), the former Muhimbili Medical Centre (1970s) and Muhimbili University College of Health Science (1991), Bugando Hospital (1970s), Bugando University College of Health Sciences, and Herbert Kairuki University as well as many other health colleges and schools are evidence of these changes. Muhimbili Orthopedic Institute (MOI) and a private heart facility at Mikocheni have played a positive role in health service delivery and improvement. An insurance system for the public that was established in the last few years is another change. The National Health Insurance Fund (NHIF) was established in 2001 and it now has 248,343 members and 3,877 facilities registered to serve the members.

This improvement is good, but it is not all that exciting. The statistics of 1960s, 1970s, 1980s and 2000s are different. They are showing improvement. But this is neither uncommon nor unexpected due to many associated changes. What I am trying to say here is that we are still far behind where we were supposed to be after 50 years.

The problems of funding, substandard facilities, poor remuneration of workers, and poor working environment have marred the health sector as much as they have other sectors. As of today, we only have 17 regional hospitals in 26 regions. We also have 70 district hospitals in more than a hundred districts. Unfortunately some of these hospitals are concentrated in only a few urban centers, such as Dar es Salaam. Dar es Salaam has a high number of special/referral, regional, and district hospitals. That leaves a very unbalanced situation despite the population distribution.

There are still many problems in providing quality service. Actually we are very far from quality service; we should first talk about sufficient service. Health services are still poor in the country. There is still a great shortage of medical personnel in comparison to the need, as well as modern working facilities. There are also irregularities in the health sector as much as in other sectors. There is still a big problem of unaccountability for instance. People still suffer and die unnecessarily because of either carelessness or irresponsibility. There has also been the persisting problem of corruption, with medical/health service personnel selling drugs on the black market when they should be safeguarding them.

There is misuse of facilities, too. Our referral hospitals are still exercising very low standards. Muhimbili has ceased being a referral hospital because even people with very minor cases or symptoms of very minor diseases that could simply be handled with any clinic choose to go to Muhimbili to get even non-prescription drugs like aspirin. This results in multitudes of patients receiving very limited services and this dilutes the quality of care altogether.

We should however commend the nongovernmental health institutions that have really helped to alleviate the health care delivery problems. Hospitals like Hindu Mandal, Aga Khan, Mikocheni (Kairuki) and other private facilities have been our refuge for health problems. But again this cannot help those who, because of poverty, are unable to afford the services offered by these facilities; hence another gap is created.

The Health Ministry has yet to develop an easy, hassle-free system for providing medical services to ordinary Tanzanians. We have heard both good and bad tales of medical care in Tanzania. There are those who spend many millions of taxpayers' money to get the best medical care in the world and the unfortunate ones who die for failure to pay a few shillings for malaria or typhoid tablets. We have also heard of those who misused government money for treatment which was never rendered to them, while others are on their death beds for want of treatment. Now, how on earth can the same poor country afford to have both groups of people: those with money to pay for no treatment and those with no money to pay for treatment? This is a problem of both ethical and moral importance. It is by nature unethical, illegal, and as such clearly unacceptable.

Health Personnel and Professionals

Like I said in the previous paragraph, there is a great shortage in our health system when we compare between what we have and what we need. For instance, our country is said to have a doctor-patient ratio of 1:25,000! That is in obviously very inadequate. The average ratios are supposed to be 1:10,000 and 1:344 for other developing and developed countries respectively. You can see where we stand.

In times past, health was defined as absence of disease or infirmity. Today – after the multidimensional definition of World Health Organization (WHO) – health is defined as the state of complete mental, physical, and social well being. Esteban Poni, in his article "Taking Charge of Your Health", on page 9 of volume 16, 2004 of *Dialogue*, a Christian magazine for college and university students, says, "aside from the physical emotional and social aspects, health also encompasses interpersonal, intellectual, and environmental dimensions." This means that health begins from knowledge and awareness. Healthy people should live in clean environments. If people are living a healthy lifestyle, they will think and act healthily and productively, and make more meaningful contributions to our communities and nations. Disease and poverty have the potential to destabilize our economy significantly, both directly and indirectly.

Unfortunately, most ordinary Tanzanians have very limited access or none at all, to good health care services. There are no reliable medical plans for low income and unemployed Tanzanians who unfortunately constitute a great portion of the society. Sound medical care is, in fact, for the privileged few. The majority cannot afford to get these services, which are actually the very basic rights of any citizen.

Due to absence of reliable medical plans to combat epidemic and contagious diseases, Tanzanians still suffer a great deal in this area. Diseases like malaria, diarrhea, cholera, tuberculosis, and typhoid have been made permanent residents in the generous land of Tanzania. Unfortunately, the most dreadful and life consuming scourge, the HIV-AIDS, has not left us alone. It has always taken lives so unfairly and in an untimely fashion. Young people whose physical and intellectual energies are so sorely needed by this country are continually perishing. As a result the life expectancy of Tanzania today is hovering around 45 years.

This is a problem that requires prompt and sustained attention. A permanent, reliable, and fair system of primary medical care should be developed, because every citizen should have access to at least primary medical care. The government needs to develop a low-cost insurance plan for low income citizens. Furthermore, it should motivate donors and large institutions to invest in the medical care industry. There are a number of ways to do this, but incentives like tax exemption or significant a reduction of some percentage offered to contributors of medical care schemes could trigger interest. The government should also take the responsibility of paying for medical insurance for those who cannot afford it.

Along with that, the Ministry of Health in collaboration with the Ministry of Women, Children, and Community Development should continue to promote healthy living in the country.

Another problem dogging this sector has been the poor incentives given to personnel. We are now used to headlines announcing strikes by doctors, nurses, students and internees. These are due to poor remuneration and they have seriously hampered the work of centers such as Muhimbili and elsewhere. That is not very shocking though. The sad aspect of the strikes is the fact that people cannot go on a death-strike, as they continue dying in the hospitals beds. The worst thing yet, is that the strikes are never given enough attention by the people in power. They come and go but people who receive pay checks to make sure the health sector is operational, whether or not they succeed, still receive their checks every month.

Diseases

HIV - AIDS

This is where the real tragedy lies. Unfortunately, the explosion of AIDS has come along with the explosion of immorality. These are two dangerous enemies to our social and economic development that have joined forces. The terrible thing is that they are both very subtle enemies. It is difficult to identify them explicitly. While immorality has disguised itself in the forms of fashions, social civilization, and rights, AIDS has sandwiched itself with sexual pleasures. These are terrible combinations, and make the situation even more threatening because they interrupt our efforts to fight them.

Of our fifty year journey, I do not recall any worse enemy of social and economic development than HIV/AIDS. As it has been rightly observed, "HIV/AIDS is no longer an issue exclusive in the Ministry of Health; but rather a multi-sectoral disaster." This is why the AIDS epidemic takes a significant part of the 50 year analysis of our independence.

For the past three decades, since the first case was reported back in 1983, Tanzania is estimated to have spent thousands of millions of shillings for the estimated more than two million funeral ceremonies caused by AIDS-related complications. Sadly, more and more people will continue to be buried as a result of HIV/AIDS complications. While statistics by Ministry of Health indicate that there were only 1.8 million people living with HIV/AIDS in Tanzania back in 2004, it was believed that there were actually more than 2.2 million people living with HIV (Business Times, June 11th 2004). *Tanzania HIV and Malaria Indicator Survey* (THMIS) 2007/08 indicates that that prevalence rate has gone down from 7% in 2003 to 5.7% in 2010, with women more affected at 6.6% compared to 4.6% for men in the 15- 49 age group.

"Different parts of the country are disproportionately affected. The prevalence of HIV infection in the mainland ranges from 1.8% in *Kigoma* region to 15.7% in *Iringa* region" as indicated in the figure below:

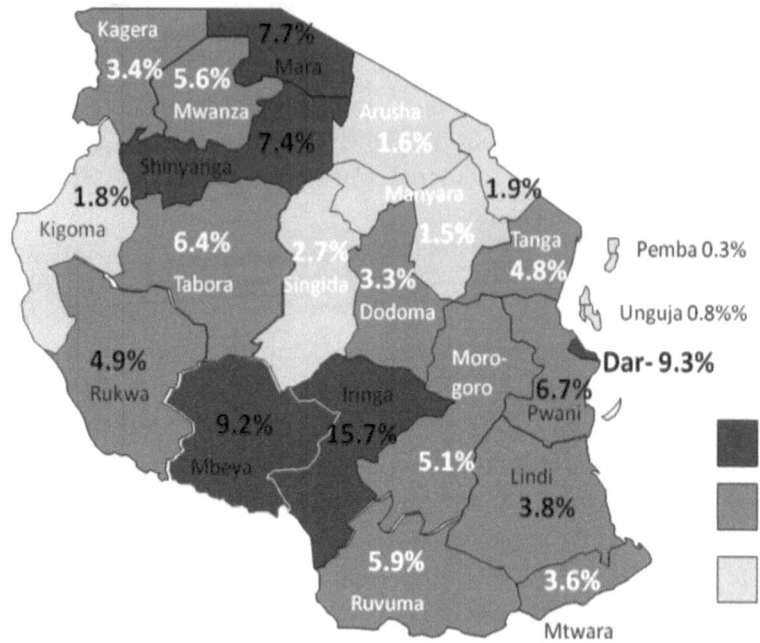

Fig. 3: HIV Prevalence in the Regions of Tanzania (Source 2007-08 THMIS)

This suggests that "The HIV epidemic in the country is driven by a complex set of intertwining biological, behavioral, and underlying socio-cultural and socio-economic factors. These factors or drivers of the epidemic comprise of multiple concurrent sexual partnerships, early sexual debut, transactional and cross-generational sex, low and inconsistent use of condoms, lack of male circumcision, sexually transmitted infection (STIs) including Herpes simplex virus type 2 (HSV-2), high levels of HIV discordance amidst low levels of knowledge of individuals' own and their partners HIV status, mobility, mother-to-child HIV transmission, low coverage of safe blood for transfusion and medical infection control precautions, gender inequities, sexual violence, harmful socio-cultural norms, socio-economic actors, drug abuse and presence of most at risk populations (MARPs) whose population size has not been determined." By HIV Prevention Review Report of Nov 2009, pg 5 – 6.

These statistics should be handled with great caution though, because it is suspected that only 1 out of 5 cases (20%) of HIV is reported. Now, this is where numbers can be very reliable. Just a simple arithmetic will help to know the neighborhood of the actual numbers. And this number is neither decreasing nor stationary. It expands exponentially every year.

This is to say that the number of deaths this year is far greater than the number of deaths last year; and the number last year is again bigger than the number the year before. This is a tragic trend!

The most disturbing fact about the consequences of HIV/AIDS is that it sweeps all the age group-from newborn babies to older people-unsparingly. It is estimated that 10% of all infected are children. It has a very undesirable pattern: people from age 0 to old age die every day, with more of them being in the group of teenage to early forties – where the strongest manpower is. Seriously speaking, if the unmarried boys and girls will not learn to zip up their pants and refrain from unprotected sexual misconduct, and if married men and women will not adopt in totality the zero-grazing discipline, the destiny of our nation is nothing but complete destruction.

There is no doubt that the deaths of thousands of citizens every year have direct consequences on the present and future economic and social development of our nation. Not only do we lose the most productive segment of human resources, but we also spend a great deal of material resources on expensive drugs and hospitalization, taking care of the orphans, unstable employment trends whereby new people are to be recruited every now and then to hold new positions. Reports indicate that the HIV/AIDS budget has swollen from Tshs. 46.07 to 597.7 billion in a period of 5 years (from 2003 – '08).

And on the other side is the horrible experience that families go through: the anguish, the shame and stigma, the frustration, and the fear that remain behind with the partners and loved ones are awful. In that regard both economic and social developments are greatly hindered.

The war against this killer disease is more or less a personal affair; but when it comes to burying citizens by the millions, it is by far more than a personal issue; that is why former President Mkapa declared AIDS as a national disaster in 1999. The government has to facilitate this war. My only concern with this issue is the amount of politics that gets into the way. The issues of abuse of human rights and personal freedom/privacy become hindrances in our efforts to counter this disease. When the people are dying in multitudes, what is the role of personal freedom and privacy? What is needed here is action, not politics! This is a situation for which we need to change some of our ways of life, at least for a short while, to help our nation survive. We should not let politics get in the way of good preventive and defensive policies.

When the government wants to accomplish its missions, some of which are not so crucial to the survival of our nation, it does not waste time discussing human rights. Neither does it consider personal freedom or privacy of its people. Brutal actions come with the label of "The Rule of Law". It is very surprising when we prefer to politicize human lives and their rights when the very human beings whose rights we want to safeguard are losing life. What do we want to keep? Is it the rights or the people? There is a very simple logic here: if we must choose one over the other, it is wise to choose keeping people instead of rights. That is to say, we can sacrifice one for a short time in order to keep both for the rest of the time.

Just out of curiosity, I happened to go through the national HIV/AIDS policy and the Tanzania Commission for Aids (TACAIDS) website. Reading it carefully, I developed an opinion that one may be tempted to think of it as an AIDS entertainment policy. The policy is seemingly being very kind to the enemy. It is as if we have come to a point of seeing AIDS as our friend and so we should learn to prepare to live with it amicably. This is a wrong approach for us to take. I think a more aggressive approach is needed at this juncture. AIDS should be fought against more vigorously than we have fought against any other disease. We need to fight it with vigor, zeal and determination, yet rightly and effectively. Attention should particularly be directed into the commitment with which the stakeholders are dealing with issues related to HIV/AIDS and more so against actions that increase the possibility of its spread.

Strict preventive and counteractive measures should be put in place. Emphasis shouldn't only be placed in the **secrecy, awareness,** and **rights** but also on preventive strategies. The situation demands that we adopt a more aggressive approach to fight the battle. This may involve going against our own normal routine of life, our traditions, or culture. In some cases we have abandoned some traditions that did not seem to conform to the level of economic or social development we have reached. To win the battle against AIDS, we may need to change our ways of thinking and doing things generally. This includes the readiness to subordinate our other interests to the task at hand. In the same note, we may even be forced to get out of our comfort zone. Therefore, human rights should not be taken as an excuse not to fight AIDS more effectively.

As indicated in the paragraph above, we need to set policies that interrupt the potential for the spread of AIDS. This should be the main focus. Section 1 of chapter 5 of the Tanzania Commission for AIDS, which is specifically about prevention, says, "The main objective is to raise the public awareness of the risk and change of behaviors that put individuals at risk of contracting or transmission of HIV or other sexually transmitted diseases in order to reduce the spread of the epidemic."

According to Tanzania HIV and Malaria Indicator Survey (THMIS) 2007/08, about 98% of all Tanzanians are aware of what HIV/AIDS is; and 60% of women and 64% of men know at least two ways of how to prevent the spread of AIDS. So this primary objective has been achieved and continues to be implemented well. Most people are now generally informed about AIDS. What they do not have is the guts to actually fight AIDS. So the biggest challenge is behavioral change, because the awareness level and the rate of behavior change are not matching.

It is also a very disturbing fact that a number of people are spreading AIDS deliberately. There are those who lost their spouses to HIV complications but keep re-marrying. There are also those who just keep multiple partners without declaring their health status, despite their condition. In reaction to that, Tanzania is becoming the first nation in Africa to have an HIV/AIDS prevention act – a law that will be against these practices.

So the step should now be to put emphasis on enforcing the laws that interrupt AIDS transmission. We will not wait until everybody is aware; some of us will be informed along the way. Afterall "some people cannot see light until they feel heat". About 10% of Tanzanians have already been infected with the HIV virus. Surprisingly, more people are affected in places where awareness is higher than places with lower levels of awareness. What this suggests is that awareness is but a small part of the war. Most people are naïve. We need to implement strict laws to affect this war.

The trend is getting worse every day; therefore more effective measures should be implemented. If anything is wrong with the strategy, we need to go back to the drawing board and revise them and be ready to change things for the better.

According to the Tanzania Commission for AIDS (TACAIDS) findings, there are a number of reported shortcomings that need to be addressed to improve the war against the spread of AIDS. These include:

Healthcare service: healthcare service, in terms of timeliness and quality, is still a far reaching phenomenon to most Tanzanians, especially in remote parts of the country where there is still a big challenge in receiving healthcare services adequately and timely. This makes it difficult for giving assistance and service to affected individuals.

Donor Dependency Budget: the budget for prevention, care and treatment (PC&T) of HIV/AIDS is heavily donor dependent (96%).

The URT government only contributes 4% of the total budget. Yet, most of the donor funds is channeled off budget, which makes it difficult to account for.

Priority and attention on issues sponsored by donor countries may shift, from time to time, to something different whenever the donors see fit. This may turn out to be catastrophic to the nation. For instance, if there is no donor fund today, this means there will be no ARV's, no salaries, and all the other associated costs for PC&T.

This, has, however been detected by the government, which intends to start an AIDS trust Fund in which TRA will be contributing percentage of its revenues for PC&T of AIDS. Other stakeholders are as well being mobilized and encouraged to participate.

Commitment: According to TACAIDS reports, commitment among stakeholders is still very low, especially in financial commitment. Funds provided for the PC&T are just considered allowances or funds for other less important projects, e.g., a social club construction project or something of the sort; and so it is for workers to spend. Workers especially at the lower level Local Government Authority (LGA) do not respect the intended purpose.

Socio-cultural Issues: there are a number of traditions that fuel transmission of HIV/AIDS. These include: Inheritance of widows; women cleansing *(women having sex with their brothers-in-law after death of the husbands)*; polygamy; and FGM *(Female Genital Mutilation)*.

Low Comprehensive Knowledge: Despite general knowledge of 98% of the population, TACAIDS has found that the comprehensive knowledge is still very low (50%) especially in villages where people still share even condoms.

Stigma and Discrimination: people still see AIDS as some kind of a curse or a disease specifically for some groups of people; so there is very little transparency within the family setting. Patients are discriminated against, and others conceal their health status to avoid stigma.

Transmission from mother to child: this is still a problem although there is quite a good progress and great hope ahead.

Blood Handling: keeping blood safe is still another challenge, more so in the villages and district hospitals.

Myths: There are still many mythical beliefs about AIDS.

MARP's (*Most At Risk Populations*): There some groups which are at higher risks, e.g., CSW's (*Commercial Sex Workers*); IDU's (Inject Drug Users); and Mine workers. Citizens in these groups need more specialized and strategic education and knowledge on AIDS and self defense.

Openness and prevention rescued Ugandans. We need to learn to be open also. Tanzanian writers are still playing the game of hide and seek in reporting deaths caused by AIDS. One has to read between the lines in order to make a guess that the person referred to actually died of AIDS. We need to loudly proclaim the truth if we mean to be serious.

Once again most people are now very well informed about AIDS. The next step should be to put emphasis on enforcing the laws that would interrupt AIDS transmission. For instance the policy remains mute about the fight against the social and socio-economic malpractices that influence the spread of AIDS.

It has been observed that many dirty and illegal activities like homosexuality being on the rise, (CSWs), (IDUs) commonly sharing needles, are going on in Tanzania, especially in Dar es Salaam, Arusha, Kilimanjaro, Mwanza, Mbeya, and Kagera that increase the potential for transmission. This is a group called concentrated epidemic group that has a high probability of acquiring AIDS. According to the Zanzibar AIDS Commission (ZAC) in a Zanzibar HIV prevalence is above 90% in the special groups mentioned above; and in the general population prevalence is persistently below 2%. This indicates that HIV/AIDS is not a generalized epidemic and needs to be fought against strategically.

And if the government is unaware of this, then the AIDS policy's main objective should be to increase government awareness of the issues that influence the spread of AIDS. Great caution should, of course, be taken in implementing the laws so as we do not micro-manage people's lives; but I believe going a little further into enforcing laws against prostitution, drug use and homosexuality will not be a big stretch. The aim is to have standards and controls that will serve to rescue innocent people who are victimized, especially the young.

Prostitution is illegal in Tanzania. But guess what? Tanzania is replete with prostitution, especially in Dar es Salaam, Arusha, Mwanza, Mbeya and Dodoma. It is not my intent to try to create an impression that prostitution is the only factor responsible for the spread of AIDS. But it is a big problem both legally and socially, and it is a sign that we are to strategize the fight. This issue is one big public concern. Prostitution is believed to be a colossal source of this deadly disease, especially when accompanied with such a great deal of sexual abuse. There is a lack of both: enforcement of laws against prostitution and laws to protect prostitutes.

The former Dar es Salaam regional Commissioner, Lieutenant (rtd) Yusuph Makamba had been reported as chasing girls around the streets at night in his personal efforts to fight prostitution. This is absurd! And it is not at all the right way to succeed in a battle like this.

Makamba's efforts were borne from his own ethical and moral standards; but the fight against AIDS is a national dilemma, an ugly dilemma. It should be a national battle. Makamba's efforts failed, and the situation is exactly what it was before his ill-fated personal crusade.

This is government playing games with its people, and in this case both the makers and breakers of the law are responsible for the evil that surrounds us. We have law makers and law enforcers; we have our police officers to help protect our society. But it is so sad to say that nothing is taken seriously. Our most menacing disease, which threatens the very survival of the nation is treated as if it were nothing, and its spread is fuelled by the inadequacy of law enforcement, which in fact is another serious problem, catalyzed by corruption and negligence. We greatly need to improve our law-enforcement system.

Sloppy slogans, like "Ajali Kazini" (accident at work) have been popularized. As much as we all know this to be a joke, we need not joke with a disease that has killed so many of our people. Even if this were in fact an accident, we still would be responsible for finding out a way to minimize it – permanently or temporarily - not cherish it.

In executing my engineering duties I've personally been exposed to many risky work environments with heavy machinery and hazardous chemicals where accidents were highly probable. In some of such environments special incentives were provided to employees as a way to minimize accidents and as a result the same dangerous environments remained accidents free for long periods of time. We have the ability to change our environments. Let's be creative and motivate people to minimize this disaster we call accident!

Another big problem that contributes to the spread of AIDS is the involvement of minors in sex abuse. School children and minors are very vulnerable in Tanzania, especially in big towns and cities. There are irresponsible adults who actually believe that sexual activities with minors is both safer and cheaper. Therefore, the latter become a target and eventually innocent victims of these crooked people. With just the least cost and minimum effort a young girl/boy is seduced into sex abuse. Again, in a country where peace is believed to belong, everyone should enjoy the peace. Therefore children should live in a secure and safe environment. This means there should be very strict laws to protect them, especially in this AIDS era, in which teenagers die of unjust causes.

Most Tanzanians know what happened to Uganda in the early and mid-eighties. Not only because we heard about it, but because after a great deal of suffering the consequences of HIV, our country started to feel the effects of the overflow. Ugandans went through a very terrible experience during these years; but guess what? Ugandans recognized and understood their problem. They declared war, and Ugandans are now much safer than most African countries such as Botswana, South Africa, Congo, Zambia, and probably Tanzania. HIV/AIDS has dropped by a huge percentage. We have a saying that goes "Ukiona mwenzako ananyolewa ..." (If you see your friend in trouble, you better get prepared. You may be next)

Surprisingly enough, we forgot about it. We saw Ugandans suffering and just sat waiting for our turn. We did not establish any cautious measures. At that time, we may claim, we had limited information about an experience so foreign to our knowledge; but the knowledge we possess today is not making much of a difference as far as counterattacking AIDS is concerned.

Apart from a sexually transmitted disease, AIDS can also be transmitted through blood transfusion and shared use of medical and nursing tools. Quite a few people have innocently been victimized in the process of getting treatment through injections or drawing of blood. There is still very poor service in terms of hygiene in some of our health stations and dispensaries. This again is a problem we need to quickly get rid of. The safety of our people is too precious to be entrusted to some few irresponsible individuals. We are capable of practicing improved and strict procedures in handling medical tools.

Tony Blair, the former British Prime Minister, in his speech on the effect of tsunami in Dec 2004, said that AIDS is man-made tsunami. He said "The tsunami was a natural disaster; but the disaster in Africa is a preventable man-made tsunami" referring to the wave of destruction that swept hundreds of thousands of people in Thailand, Sri Lanka, India, Indonesia, and other parts of the world in late December 2004. By his observation AIDS is a preventable and controllable disease. I guess my opinion is along the same line of thought.

We should refuse to die carelessly; at least not of AIDS, and at least not all of us.

My suggestion in this area is a two-fold approach. First, joining the entire world against this disease, we should adopt a general approach such as suggested and used by other countries, WHO, and anti-AIDS groups. There have been many suggested measures on a global level. These include abandoning silly traditions, emphasis on one-man-one-woman (or, rather, two partner) marriages, faithfulness between partners, regular medical checkups, and the most common: regular use of male, and recently, female condoms. The international community has given physical contribution in monetary terms and in material forms and human resources. The USA, under Presidents Bill Clinton and later George W. Bush, gave significant financial support to Uganda, Tanzania and other heavily affected areas. In 1998, for instance, this aid amounted to US$ 45.6m (Tshs. 46b then) as a support to the war against AIDS. More tangible contribution was through a global fund from developed countries in an effort to control malaria, TB, and HIV/AIDS in developing countries. The use of ARVs was emphasized in this program. To that extent, the international community may be doing its share of the task.

At another level, we also need to come up with a more specific approach that is suitable to the surroundings of our own country. It should be remembered that despite this disease posing a global threat, it has different levels of impact on different societies/countries. Such things as economy level, culture, social life-styles, traditions, and natural laws may be potential stimulants and/or channels for the spread of AIDS and they differ significantly from society to society and from one nation to another. Therefore it is also significant that we, as Tanzanians, come up with a unique approach for our country. We need to seriously review our cultural practices, traditions, and even national laws to isolate those which contribute to the spread of AIDS, and the findings should not remain hidden in paper reports and proposals in seminars and workshops, but should be translated and implemented seriously and practically.

Furthermore, this should result in better and more localized medical and scientific research that may yield solutions compatible with our surroundings. Our medical personnel should be encouraged to employ a more innovative approach to fight against AIDS including the use of traditional medicine and natural cure options. Natural cures have proven to be very effective in most cases and have minimal side effects. Most people in other countries are now turning back to natural cures because of fewer side effects. Therefore research activities in both scientific and traditional medicine should be promoted.

The availability of life prolonging drugs (ARVs) seemed to be such "good news" to some people; but it is sad to say that the introduction of those medicines is in fact a mixed package – it has both positive and negative implications. I am particularly concerned with the negative: if the control programs remain poor, people will use the medicines unfavorably. If for instance one ill-intended person who can afford the medicine wants to spread the disease, she has a better chance now than before, taking into consideration the fact that these medicines do not cure, but suppress the visible symptoms for a while.

By using the medicine this person prolongs life, which is of course everybody's desire; but during this time of prolonged life facts show that symptoms may be hidden. Dishonest people can abuse our efforts in the fight and more people are at higher risk than before, considering especially that this disease affects the mental faculty of a human being too. That means the thought process worsens and the decision making becomes affected. Therefore an affected person can make very unpredictable decisions and that heightens the level of risk to others.

This is far from saying that we should not care for the AIDS patients, but rather this is trying to say that we have to fight AIDS and not entertain it. In doing this, there might be some interference in so-called personal freedom and privacy but people should be prepared to understand, cooperate, and accommodate this. This is of course one way to take part in the fight, and if the purpose is for the benefit of the general public, it is worth the interference, after all that is as tragic as it can get; but continuing to be lax can be overwhelmingly dangerous.

So, the administration of the fourth phase government should emphasize these local measures to fight against AIDS. I deeply regret to say that the last administration did not put much emphasis on science and technology enhancement. There apparently were no efforts to encourage scientific researches and technology not only in medical careers but also in every specialty.

The modern world economy is technology-based. Talking about economic development means the advancement of technology. Technology advancement and economic development are so married together that thinking of either without the other is almost incomprehensible. This leaves us with few optional choices, but starting to deliberately encourage scientific researches to help development of technology, which will eventually make a way for our economy to improve.

Tuberculosis

March 24th every year the World Health Organization (WHO) marks the World TB Day. This is normally intended for going back to records of the effects and impact of TB on individual countries as well as globally. It is also set aside for measures to be taken on the fight against TB; and according to the World Health Organization, "Tanzania is reported to rank fourth among the 22 high TB burden countries in the world". This means we are in a more serious situation than it looks.

Table 2: The Trend of TB between 1990 – '09

Year	No. of Patients
1990	22,249
1991	25,210
1992	28,462
1993	31,460
1994	34,378
1995	39,003
1996	43,799
1997	46,636
1998	51,231
1999	52,437
2000	54,582
2001	61,625
2002	63,060
2003	63,211
2004	64,665
2005	66,400
2006	65,600
2207	62,800
2008	63,600
2009	61,600

Source: Ministry of Health (TB and Leprosy Control Program)

It is clear that among many other diseases, tuberculosis has claimed a good portion of Tanzanian lives. The situation has been worse in the recent past since TB comes as an ally of HIV-AIDS. Tuberculosis may surface among the symptoms of HIV. After the body's immunity declines, chances are higher that a person may contract TB; and TB comes in many forms, which is why TB has increasingly killed more people after the explosion of AIDS in the country. It's been observed that "Annually, about 2600 Tanzanians die of TB. The increased burden of TB in Tanzania is being fueled by HIV/AIDS." (Ngadaya 2009)

Statistics from the National TB and Leprosy Control Program (NTLP) of the Ministry of Health indicate that between 1990 and 2005 (with the highest number of cases) there was an increase of about 198.44% in TB cases. There were 22,249 recorded cases in 1990 and by 2005 the number of cases rose to over 66,400 recorded cases.

However, according to the Ministry of Health, the rate of increase was not the same in the past decade. The rate went down; subsequent observations have indicated that the number of TB cases in the country has consistently remained below 64,000 up to 2011.

Table 2 summarizes the situation of TB for the 20 years since 1990 in our country.

Leprosy

"Leprosy is a special public health problem as it is still an important cause of permanent disabilities and continues to have a very negative social image in the community, frequently responsible for discrimination and stigmatization." Ministry of Health – Tuberclosis and Leprosy Programme website.

"There was a time, not long ago, when to be afflicted with leprosy was to face death, preceded by social ostracism. People were very much afraid of leprosy to the extent of excluding those who were suffering." (Julius K. Nyerere, Freedom and Socialism, 1968). Thanks to advances in medical science and those who devoted their efforts to this field, leprosy is now cured. "Actually if diagnosed timely, chances are high that even the terrible disfigurements associated with it can be avoided".

Leprosy services are provided free of charge within the general health care services but are coordinated by the TB/Leprosy coordinators at all levels.

Multiple Drug Therapy (MDT), the cornerstone of leprosy control, was introduced in the Tanzania National TB/Leprosy Programme in 1983 and reached countrywide coverage in 1990. This resulted in a rapid decline of the number of registered leprosy cases under treatment from nearly 35,000 cases in 1983 to about 3500 in the year 2006.Tanzania reached the leprosy elimination targets in 2006. Currently, the registered prevalence of leprosy is 0.9/10,000" (www.moh.go.tz).

A number of leprosariums in Mtwara, Shinyanga, etc., have an important role in this positive development. The statistics by the Ministry of Health indicate that we had 7,007 case of leprosy in 2002 and this number has been dropped to 5,771 by 2003 – a decrease of 21.42%. By 2009 there were less than 3000 cases. This number has, however, increased from the numbers we had in 1964 – 1965 around 700 cases, but the situation is not that scary when we consider the population growth over the same period of time. The numbers were bouncing at the lower 3000's in 2010 and are now even less. Bravo to medical personnel for this progress, although we have to keep it up.

Fig. 4 shows the trend of Leprosy in the past 20 years as indicated on NTBLP report of 2009.

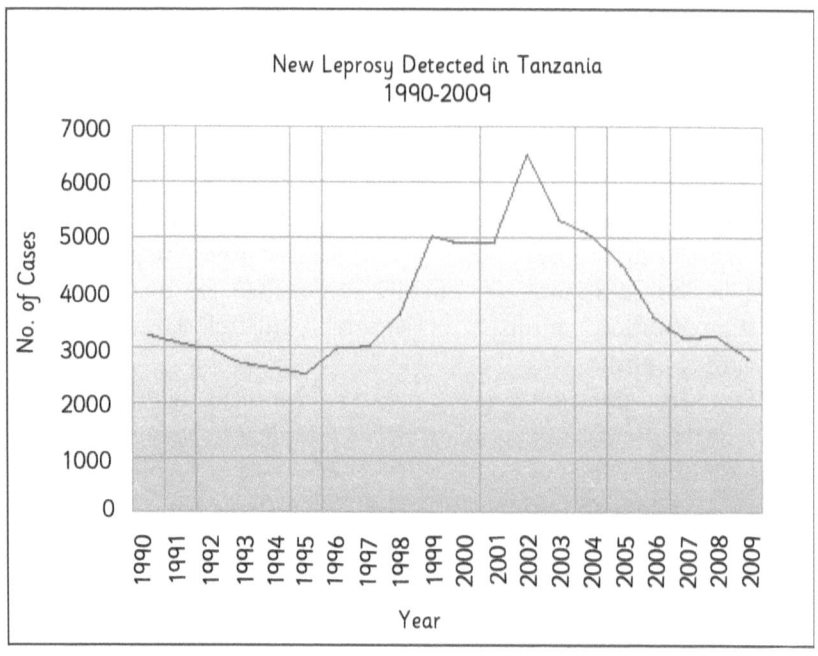

Fig. 4: The Status of Leprosy in Tanzania

Cancer

Cancer has become another global threat, and Tanzania has not been spared. Each year there are over 20,000 new patients with cancer in Tanzania. Currently, the Ocean Road Cancer Institute (ORCI) can treat only about 2,500 patients per year - only a fraction of radiotherapy needs in Tanzania. With its numerous types and levels, cancer is a real problem. Cancer is said to be "the second most common cause of death worldwide after cardiovascular disease. Over 7 million people died of cancer in 2005, and close to 11 million new cancer cases were diagnosed," This is according to the World Health Organization (WHO).

Just as with TB, the advent of AIDS has increased the incidences of most other diseases. AIDS kills immunity, weakening the body and making it prone to risk of attack from different diseases. Progress has been registered here too, but we cannot allow ourselves to be complacent. We are yet to reach a point at which we can relax.

The government managed to found an institution that specifically deals with cancer patients - Ocean Road Cancer Institute (ORCI), and other private cancer institutions have been established. However, the situation is still getting worse in terms of the reported number of cancer cases.

The common types of cancer that we are struggling with include breast cancer, cervical cancer, prostate cancer, and most recently blood cancer (leukemia) and many others. Leukemia is a threat – a big threat, not only to Tanzanians but the world over. Our historic records from the Ministry of Health and elsewhere do not indicate the existence of this Lukemia. It is a recent phenomenon, but it also has robbed us of our loved ones. Leukemia is said to claim a good portion of the Tanzanian population, and it is on the rise.

Breast cancer is said to be very prevalent. More than 10% of women who were involved in a survey by the women doctors' association in 2005 were found with this type of cancer. This is according to the Medical Women Association of Tanzania website.

Prostate cancer is also growing very rapidly. Even scarier is the fact that cervical cancer has perhaps caused more deaths than all the other types combined.

But the good news is that these days cancer is curable if diagnosed early enough, meaning that regular checkups are very important because in some cases cancer tends to hide a long time before giving signs of its presence.

Malaria

I was, at one time, traveling back home – Tanzania, and when we were about to land on the "Heaven of Peace" the pilot informed us about the landing and also cautioned us that we were coming to the country that has a lot of malaria! Not only was I surprised but I was a little disturbed. It sounded like ridicule, but I later remembered that we were so used to living with malaria that we no longer considered malaria to be a frightening disease, but it really is.

Other diseases take a back seat to malaria, which is the number one killer in Tanzania. It has killed our people for many years. It is estimated that malaria kills an average of about 100,000 Tanzanians each year – that means one person dies every five minutes. More startling is the fact that among these deaths 70% are children under five.

In 2002 malaria cases were said to be five times higher than those from HIV, leprosy, TB and small pox combined. Unfortunately in all these decades we have not found an effective and permanent method to get rid of the chief responsible agent (mosquitoes). We live with mosquitoes, we sleep with mosquitoes, we work with mosquitoes and they have been sucking our blood mercilessly.

Malaria is estimated to be responsible for the death of more than 10 million people in the past fifty years. Nothing has ever caused as much damage to our country as malaria. Recent study indicates that the persistence of the malaria parasites is growing. Most processed drugs that were used to cure malaria are no longer effective. That's bad news! But another good reason to go back to our natural cures and things like mu-arobaini. Incidentally, experiments are underway now to try to make a stronger combination of drugs. Dawa Mseto is a result of the efforts to come up with a stronger combination against Malaria parasites.

Another effort that has been made by the malaria control program is the distribution anti-mosquito nets. This is a commendable effort, but we have to remember this is only a temporary preventive measure. We need to completely eradicate malaria with more scientific methods.

Small-Pox

This is another disease which the Ministry of health has dealt with rather more successfully. Small pox is under control. Statistics indicate that there were 3,027 cases of small pox in 1964. We had no reported case by August 1970. This was excellent. Till now, small pox has been well controlled. It has not been among the biggest troubles of our nation lately.

Polio

We no longer have findings of polio.

Typhoid

With its undisclosed symptoms, typhoid has also been a big threat lately. It has been the cause of death in many cases. It seems, in some cases, poor health service is a big contributing factor. According to medical opinion, typhoid fever is one of the easiest diseases to control when diagnosed in its early stages. Poor facilities in Tanzania make it a difficult problem and in many cases it is not diagnosed until it is too late. It is difficult to distinguish specifically by statistics but general conclusions indicate that typhoid is on the rise.

Hypertension
This is among the man-made diseases of the 20th century. With exceptions of aging, pregnancy, and probably heredity, most heart/blood-related problems are lifestyle-related. Our attitudes toward food and physical exercises are very closely connected to heart disease.

As I mentioned earlier in my discussion of the WHO multi-dimensional definition of health, it is not just the absence of disease, it is rather the total well being. Knowledge of our bodies is a vital factor for healthy living. Hypertension has turned out to be one of the big life-threats to our country these days, and it is responsible for the numerous sudden deaths of our people especially those in high positions of white-color jobs. It is unfortunate that this problem has no definite cure but proper use of control drugs has been emphasized, although it is important to know that a patient's health is more related to her individual lifestyle.

Spinal Meningitis
Here is to be found another subtle enemy. Meningitis is another problem which in many cases eludes detection by Tanzania's poor health equipment and expertise. Its nefarious effects have been felt especially since the late eighties. Again, the major problem lies in the fact that it comes in a disguised form and many a times goes unnoticed until it brings ruin. Not enough data is provided here to show the trend, but general observation tells us that meningitis has killed a good number of people in Tanzania.

Epidemics
Epidemical diseases have made many frequent stops to our country. Dar es Salaam has probably faced a greater risk of epidemics due to its high density population and various environmental factors in some areas. The sad part of the story is that most of these diseases, cholera being the worst and the most frequent, are associated with cleanliness (or the lack thereof) and could easily be controlled if we chose to live in clean surroundings. This is just a matter of choice; we do not need any expatriates to come and tell as how to live hygienically. But the issue of hygiene is still a big social issue. Sanitation and waste management systems are poorly designed and operated and hence are risks of such diseases. I am not even considering this as among the government problems in our fifty years, but rather it is a result of our total negligence.

Education

Down the ages, education has meant different things to different generations. At one time education meant only investigation, classification, and communication of physical and natural phenomena, influenced greatly by human philosophical reasoning. At another time education meant adhering to Biblical principles and guidance, at which time any form of secular education was deemed unacceptable. Now with modern civilization, a new form of education based on science, technology, and ethical living has been made indispensable.

Tanzania, as part of the modern world cannot choose but to accede to this type of learning. The administrations of all the three phases of government have invested appreciably and tried to make sure that we have enough schools and colleges. However there are still questions that are important here: one, Have we done everything we can, to improve our education? And two, Are we where we are supposed to be fifty years down the road? To answer these questions, and others, we have to examine both the numerical and qualitative sides of our efforts in the education sector.

Tremendous progress has been made in the education system since independence with regard to construction of the number of schools and college levels as well as the number of students attending and graduating today. Literacy percentile scales have greatly increased (from 25% in 1964 about 95% in the 1970s before again a significant decline to about 65% in the 1980s and early 1990s) and more teachers, local tutors, and instructors have been trained during this period. It is my intention to highlight these areas, but also to attempt an in-depth discussion of the quality of our education, as well as point out some of the glaring shortcomings.

Education Setting

When Tanganyika and Zanzibar merged to form the United Republic of Tanzania, they both had undergone the colonial master's education system. It was, therefore, not surprising that the new nation inherited the old system, although with some tinkering. We have, however, gone through a number of transitions since then. Some changes had to be effected in order to respond to the needs of the times and what were perceived as being the real objectives of our education system.

These changes put into consideration the objectives and methods of our education with respect to time. In the early sixties we changed from 8(4 yrs of lower primary and 4 yrs of upper primary) – 4 – 2 – 3 to 8(4 yrs of lower primary, 2 yrs of extended primary, and 2 yrs of upper primary) – 4 – 2 – 3; and in 1968, 8 years of primary education were reduced to 7 and established a 7 - 4- 2 *(4 yrs of lower primary and 3 yrs of upper primary, 4 of ordinary level secondary school, 2 of advanced level sec school)* a reduction of one year. Some years later, the standard-four examination was dropped, perhaps because of the high drop-outs of pupils at this level, and as a result we remained with only one continuous segment of 7 years of primary education. After the seven years a pupil goes to the secondary level, which comprises 4 years of "Ordinary" level secondary school, and 2 years of "Advanced" level school. After that came the tertiary level, with duration of three to five years. It is thus that today, a Tanzanian student has to spend at least 17 years in schooling to obtain a college degree with a number of exams – standard-seven exam, form-two exam, forms four and six exams

Fifty years down the road – do we still need to continue with this system of education? I am not very sure, but analysis in this section, backed up by a comparison with other systems of education will highlight how others spend less time in school and come out equally or better trained than we do. However, what I am trying to concern myself with here is not how long our children spend, or should spend in school, but rather the quality of education achieved when children leave school.

Progress in Education

As stated earlier, Tanzanian education has grown impressively in terms of increase in numbers of schools (primary/elementary, secondary and high schools), vocational schools, colleges, universities, and other higher learning institutions and the number of students attending and graduating from these schools and colleges at different levels. The number of primary schools has increased from about 3,800 in 1964 to 13,689 in 2004. We now have 1,291 secondary schools as compared to the very few back at the time of the union. In 1964, we had 747,000 children between the ages of six and eight being enrolled in primary schools yearly. 75% of them would be eliminated by the grade-four exam. The corresponding numbers in 2010 was well over seven million.

In 1966 there were 4,700 form four graduates as compared to 98,294 in 2004 in both private and public schools. There were 760 form six graduates in 1996, compared to 31,001 in 2004 (Ministry Education). We had one university under the East Africa University system that enrolled a total of 887 (by 1967) students from Tanzania. There were over twenty fully-fledged universities and associate universities in 2010. According to the Ministry of Science, Technology and Higher Education's 2004/05 financial budget, the total of university students in public universities in 2004 was 28,910 and 2,731 in private universities. This was about 12% increment as compared to the year before.

Special programs, e.g., adult education, Universal Primary Education (UPE), Musoma Resolution (1975) and others, especially the most recent and probably more effective Primary Education Development Plan (PDEP) have also been good part of the efforts to have a learned people. With these endeavors, the literacy level has increased by a good percentage. Education policy has changed for the better.

But then we have to view these numbers and statistics with great caution because we are comparing almost totally two different generations: a 12-million-person generation with a 2.7% growth rate and an over 35-million-person generation with over 3% growth rate, an increase of almost 200% in population.

Primary Education

One of the priorities of the first phase government was education for all. The late Mwl. Nyerere placed much emphasis on educating not only children, but also adults who had missed the opportunity. In the seventies, Tanzania made commendable progress in primary education, and by 1980 the goal to enroll every child of school-going age was 100% achieved. However, economic crises of the early 1980s greatly hampered these efforts of expansion of primary school enrollment. School dropouts increased. Enrollment fell due to the re-introduction of school fees in mid -80s/90s. According to the Ministry of Education, by 1995 Gross Enrollment Ratio (GER) dropped to 67.7% and the National Enrollment Ratio (NER) to 58%. This was a huge setback, but certainly not the only one.

In his paper on the direction of primary education at the University Convocation (2003), Rakesh Rajani of Haki-Elimu, an education advocacy NGO, there is also a problem of inequality in enrollment between rural and urban children that seemed to be alarming. Between 1995 and 2000, for instance, Rajani indicated that there was 15% higher enrollment in urban areas than rural areas. "Differences between districts are even greater. In 2000, while about 94% of school-age children were enrolled in Kibaha and 87% in Ilala, the comparative figures for Lindi and Ngorongoro were 28% and 37% respectively."

According to Rajani, "perhaps even more startling were the differences within districts." He indicated that studies from 1999 and 2000 revealed large disparities." Giving Temeke as an example, he indicated that Somangila and Kurasini had a Net Enrollment Ratio (NER) of between 80% and 90% while Tandika and Mjimwema had only 27% and 15%

respectively. Balanced development between urban and rural areas is an important criterion in economic development. In sharp contrast to what is happening with the given data, it is clearly shown that there is still so much disparity.

These are real problems right there. Leaving as much as 85% of school-age children without accessibility to education is a time bomb about to explode. Despite the obviously beneficial reforms that have been undertaken by the third phase leadership under PEDP there are still major problems, fifty years down the road to the Promised Land, still waiting for our attention. Many other things still need changing.

There is, for instance, a problem of lack of provision of appropriate resources to disabled children. Now, this is a country that is said to have more than 4.5% children, of the entire Tanzanian population today, who are mentally or physically disabled, and who need and deserve quality social services, education being among the most basic and the most useful. Failure to provide for these children is an important impediment to our efforts to care for the most vulnerable members of our society.

But one of the most important and practical development strategies of the third phase government in this area was the implementation of the five-year Primary Education Development Plan (2002-2006).

Tanzania started implementing the Universal Education Sector Development Program (UESDP) in 2002 by implementing PEDP, which had four major objectives:
- Expansion of Enrolment
- Improvement of quality
- Capacity building
- Establishment of Strength institutional arrangements

After the adoption of PEDP in 2002 changes were obvious. In 2003 Std 1 GER was boosted to 100% once again with a total enrollment of 1.6 million children. In 2004 the reports by PEDP were more impressive when a GER of 108.3% (*in comparison to 2001 before introduction of PEDP*) and an NER of 90.4% were achieved. PEDP did more than just enroll pupils. By 2004, just two years after its implementation, achievements that were recorded included: 1,081 new primary schools were built; 31,825 classrooms and 7,530 teachers' houses were built with the help of donors and community development projects; and 17,854 new teachers were recruited while 14852 others were retrained. Availability of text books has improved from a ratio of 1:8 to 1:3 in Class I – IV; and from 1:10 to 1:6 in Class V – VII. The pass rate of the Primary School Leaving Examination has risen from 22% in 2001 to 40.1 per cent in 2003.

Secondary Education

In 2003 12.3% GER and only 7 – 8.4% NER were recorded in secondary school enrollment – form one to form four. The NER was 5% in 1995. There is a great demand for the same measures that were taken in improving primary education to be implemented here too. And of course there is good news - "The Government started implementing the Secondary Education Development Plan (SEDP) 2004-2009 which aimed at improving quality of secondary education and expansion of enrollment to NER of 50% by 2010, which entails an increase of students from 430,000 in (2004) to 2,000,000 by 2010." As of 2001 about 91,119 (among 444,903) who graduated from primary schools were enrolled in secondary schools. That is about 20.5% of those who graduated. Again, in a world where a college degree is considered as basic education, leaving about 80% of students with only elementary education and many others without any formal education is a form of extreme injustice.

Quality of Education

Quality, taken in an ordinary context, may be explained as something to do with distinctiveness or excellence in methodology, relevance, and usefulness. Usefulness means the ability to satisfy the implied or stated needs. Relevant education here is defined as a set of skills that meets the growing demands of advancement of science and technology in the highly paced and modernized world. According to this criterion our education may still be way behind what may be considered quality education. One problem that has persisted during the entire fifty years is the shortage of funding, the result of which we now have a shortage of manpower, a shortage of facilities, and a shortage of good learning surroundings, hence a lack of quality education.

Funding

According to the working paper number 2003.2 on the implementation of PEDP by Japhet Makongo, also of Haki-Elimu, one of the most important components of PEDP is the commitment to ensure significantly that adequate funds reach the school level for quality improvements and the "Capitation Grant" of $10 per pupil per year ($6 in cash and $4 worth of learning materials) was the main device to achieve this. $10 (about Tshs. 16,000) is a very little amount of money to associate with quality improvement in the 50th year along the road to the Promised Land. Quality improvement includes teaching, purchase of good and modern books, desks, chalks, boards, control of examinations, and other costs – 10 dollars is not enough, period. Yet more surprisingly, according to recent reports in many cases schools have received only $2 of these funds per pupil. $2 being allocated to finance one of the most important needs of a civilized society – this is most disturbing! There is a serious problem here. Just think about it in a different way – you hold $2 in the right hand and a pupil's budget for the year in the left hand – and you are still uttering words like education, quality, improvement, success – something is just not right here. The only four words that would make sense in the given scenario would be, "there is a tragedy."

Resources

Another major shortcoming in our education system has been shortage of resources, both human and material. For many years we have had an acute shortage of teaching and administrative staff in our schools. There are schools with a single teacher. One person – *I know that does not make sense, does it?* But it is a fact. Halima Jamal, newspaper writer, wrote from Itigi on Tanzania Daima on July 23rd 2011, on the risk of the only teacher of *Mukajenga Primary School*, at Ipande, West Manyoni Constituent, running away because of nonpayment of his 10 month salary arrears. Other (secondary) schools that have been reported to have single teachers include *Marambo Secondary School in Nachingwea*, Lindi which was said to have more than 250 students (Habari Leo, 20th April 2009); *Mizengo Pinda Secondary School* in Mpanda, Rukwa (Tanzania Daima, 1st August 2009); etc.

Our average student-teacher ratios in primary schools have gotten as bad as 80:1 in some areas in recent years; but we have also seen primary school classes with 200 students listening to one teacher! That is a disgrace. Schools have been known to close simply because one teacher was ill. Now in a country that suffers so much from malaria and cholera, as we have seen above, how many closures shall we have in a year simply because one teacher has reported sick? And more importantly how many days shall remain for our children to learn?

Shortage of teachers afflicts secondary schools as well. The same applies to our college instructors where there is a huge demand for qualified teaching staff. We need much more improvement if we are to reach our target. The good news is we can do it.

Material resources have been an even worse problem. We have experienced a shortage of books and other teaching materials, as well as desks, and even the most fundamental unit of academic life, a classroom, has been a big problem. Many smart and very bright students spend at least seven years of their academic life under the shade of trees, changing from under one tree to another depending on the convenience of the teacher, the direction of the shade as a result of the position of the sun, and what kind of a bird is on the tree that time of the day. Thank the Lord, "God keeps away flies for tailless animals"; we happen to have no tornados, hurricanes, winter, or hot summers in Tanzania.

Even those who are lucky enough to be within four walls are rained on and have had to endure hot sun at least some of times. And those who are even luckier to have all the five sides, four walls and the roof, had no place to sit – some sat on the dust, some on the cold or hot cement floors. There are those who attend schools with decent classroom buildings, but guess what? – no books.

One of the important criteria on education is the curriculum. While globalization requires education that can be useful universally, emphasis should be put on meeting local priorities. The dilemma that faces our country today is that most people are trained in foreign institutions where the education they obtain remains, to a greater part, as a set of theories that are hard to practice locally because they lack relevance.

Another dilemma is the emphasis of what is no longer needed and the neglect of what is most important. Life changes very fast, therefore the demands and priority of things also change with equal pace, but our curriculum in education has remained static for many years. We need to change, and continue changing. The economic and social changes that occurred in the 1990s were too much to accommodate the same system of education that has been there thirty to fifty years without changes.

Frustration sets in when people end up with far less than they expected. For instance, for the most part, our education was meant to provide preparation for people to become loyal employees. In the early 1990s great changes occurred in the entire employment configuration, and ever since people have been forced to find employment in private sectors or in self-employment, in an environment where almost everything was left to competition in the free market; many of our young graduates were not adequately prepared for this drastic paradigm shift.

This was obviously another major error. People who have spent most of their time in school to make good grades in order to impress their potential employers can not all of sudden be told to simply employ themselves. They have been trained to be good employees – not employers. It is, therefore, obvious that they cannot just become the best at being self-employed. There must have been a change in the systems and attitudes in which these people are to function; but in the absence of such change it is hardly surprising that our economy has performed as poorly.

It is thus high time we take a little break and review our education system once again, with a view to affecting a major rehabilitation. There are no employers out there, therefore the emphasis and the focus of our education should change. The least a person should expect from education is to receive training that will help her survive in the world of competition and stand the challenges of the world of the so-called free market.

Some of the socialist theories cannot hold water any more at this point, so far down the road of capitalistic ways of life. People have complained for instance, that Nyerere taught us that money was not the basis of development. I am not sure about the situation then, but for now, the bottom line is money. Money is almost everything when it comes to a better life economically. If we are to educate people, we need to let them know how to survive in the "money world" because we have seen very well that money is power in the world today. The bottom line is: education should serve the individual and collective needs of the people and the nation. Short of that education is meaningless. We cannot keep on learning while getting worse socially, economically, and professionally as days go by.

To prepare our people for better quality lives as individuals, we need to set our priorities straight: money-related subjects like accounts, economics, and finance in which emphasis should put on capital sources, taxation, banking, assets, liability, stock and financial markets must become important subjects and probably should be made compulsory for every student regardless of the school of attendance and the student's area of specialization. I have personally been in school for almost 20 years; but during all this time, nobody taught me, at any stage of my education how to make and spend money. If I had not taken an extra-curricular interest of my own I would have never known how to read a financial statement; the reason being simply that I went to a technical school and I was reading to become an engineer. But engineers need to make money. Now if I cannot know the basics of making money, what was it that I was going to school for and in which society would I fit? The old school of thought of Nyerereism, which sought to convince us that if you taught people how to make money you would be encouraging dishonesty should be done away with in today's world in which everything seems to revolve around money.

Instructional Medium
There is a serious but neglected or undermined concern of the significance of medium of instruction to our education system. Since the mid-1970s researchers, commentators, commissions and academicians have suggested a need to re-consider the question of a medium of instruction in our school system especially at post-elementary level. On the other hand the government has remained firm with the use of English as

the medium of instruction at a secondary school level and above. A recent outbreak of international schools has given a few children an opportunity to learn English from lower levels and hence present an unfair competition to their counterparts, whose parents never had the means to put them in the "international school system".

A great majority of Tanzanians has very little use of English. This poses a query of the rationale of having Kiswahili as a national language and used by almost everybody versus English, which is used by only 5% of the Tanzanian population (Schmied, 1989), being the medium of instruction in education. In any case this concern seems legitimate due to the struggle the students have to manage English with minimal preparation.

Tanzania has more than 120 vernaculars and Kiswahili as a national language and the most widely used language outside the classroom environment. Some pupils start at home with the use of their vernacular, then switch to the use of Kiswahili in their primary education and finish up with English. While this trend gives students an advantage of being introduced to many languages in a very short span, it is the assassin of the ability to gain a good mastery of any of the languages well enough for good grades in school.

Kiswahili is used as the medium of instruction at primary level education. This means that most children are highly exposed to the Kiswahili language both inside and outside the classroom. Studies indicate a very direct correlation between language of instruction in the education system and the students' performance in class activities.

At secondary level an abrupt change occurs when students start using English as the medium of instruction. Studies have indicated that standards have dropped in direct relation with the mastery of the language. Zaline M. Roy-Campbell and Martha A.S. Quorro in their book *Language Crisis in Tanzania, The Myth of English versus Education* published by Mkuki na Nyota (1997) suggest that there is a need to seriously review the issue of medium of instruction. On pages 3 and 4 of the book we find the following:

> Throughout the 1970s and 1980s there was mounting concern, both public and professional, over the apparent fall in the standard of English among secondary and post-secondary school students in Tanzania. The problem appeared to be related with the fact that while Kiswahili was the national language of Tanzania and the medium of instruction for primary schools, English was the instructional medium for post-primary school education. Failure to achieve adequate competence in English in order to use it effectively as a medium of education appeared to result in

poor performance in school, as pupils showed very little understanding of what was presented to them in their school courses.

This book continues to suggest that:

One of the channels through which much of post-primary school education is transmitted is reading. Pupil's inability to cope with the demands of the school curriculum because of their inability to read and understand materials related to their studies appeared to be one result of the fall in standards of English.

With reference to many researches, studies and publications, Campbell and Quorro made a suggestion that I think has merit and may be of help as people consider the situation of academics and the medium of instruction. Their concluding remarks are that for Tanzania to get out of this crisis of language, few options are available to us: one, to return English as medium of instruction in primary school so students may have a good and strong background and therefore mastery of the English language; two, formalizing bilingual education in secondary schools where teachers and students may have the option of choice of language they want to use in instruction or writing tests and exams; and three, to change everything in secondary and college education into Kiswahili.

All the options have their pros and cons as discussed in the book at lengthy, but nothing seems to impress the administration of our country, which has continually and very rigidly chosen to keep the option that has practically been very ineffective.

A Computer World

It has rightly been observed that computer technology is probably the most important discovery ever made by man. Besides, computers will impact different aspects of our lives more extensively than did the automobile, the printing press, the telephone, radio and TV combined! The computer has even necessitated new vocabularies in different languages. Some words have changed meanings and new words have been formulated as a response to the impact of the computer technology. We cannot over-emphasize the importance of computers in our lives today.

Computers are everything today. Computers are everywhere, and computers do everything. They make planes and fly them (Little did I know that some of these planes flying over our heads use auto-piloting, some with no human pilots, just controlled by computer systems in some situations). This sounded so scary to me when I discovered it. But the level of technology and precision reached by computer technology seems to be almost unfailing.

Computers make cars and computers build houses. They are in the banks and in the markets. They are in schools and in hospitals. They teach people and treat people. They employ and pay. They hire and fire. They are in workplaces and in courtrooms. They have replaced many people and many things, and they have simplified many jobs. They can send a mail in an instant. They can talk and they can sing. They can draw and they can paint. The world has reached a level of technology where funeral arrangements are now made through computer internet systems. Refrigerators are nowadays more than just storage devices. New models with data and signal transfer capability will soon be available. These models can be connected to a supermarket with computer network systems and send data on the status of the groceries and arrange a new order and delivery whenever the groceries are out of stock in a particular customer's address so customers, while busy with their careers, need never worry about the groceries in their homes or even about going to the grocery stores.

Therefore computer knowledge these days is as indispensable as it is dynamic, and that is why our curriculum should be made to accommodate such a crucial requirement of the modern world and keep abreast of its rapid development.

Computers should not only be used to decorate classrooms in schools. Pupils should be taught how to use them efficiently and productively. Computer knowledge should be a compulsory course in our schools. Pupils should learn computers from a very early grade level.

In this age of information technology, another area that needs our special attention is that of communication skills, which should also be accorded high priority. We should quickly shift from the old notions of putting emphasis on engineering and basic scientific subjects only and move on to a balanced society. As the world becomes a village competition becomes an unavoidable reality especially, as Stephen Covey, 2004 said in his book *7 Habits of Highly Effective People*, "the basic view of success shifted from character ethics to personality ethics. Success became a function of personality." What he meant here is that those things that lubricate the process of human interaction (communication being the most important) are as essential as the knowledge of engineering and science.

In recent years Tanzanians are said to have had a difficult time competing with fellow East Africans in the job and business markets of the region. Surprisingly this statement was given by a person who, as senior government leader, should somehow be accountable for that situation. The situation is worse in the outer world. Most Tanzanian students have a difficult time communicating. Even those who made good grades in school and went as far as having MBAs and PhDs do not do so well when it comes to competing in the professional world. Now that the market is flooded with professionals, the only way to survive is to compete. How do we compete? Selling our products, which are - our credentials.

Marketing and advertising have been proven to be very effective in increasing sales of any business. Having a good product alone will not get you very far. Advertising the product is an important step in selling it. It goes without saying, therefore, that however important our grasp of science, engineering and others we need to hone our communication skills because it is through them that we get to make the world know what we know and can do.

I also find it important to make a comparison of education system to that of our neighbors and to other nations. With our system a student spends six years of secondary education before joining college. Our neighbors in Kenya have done away with the "A-levels" as have many other countries, which opted for only four years of secondary education. The products of this system have been known to compete equally well or better than us in the career and business market in the world. If anything, one would have thought that we would have had an added advantage because of the two extra years in our system. If there is no demonstrable advantage to be had from our six-year system, then why do we not scrap it? If by lesser means we can reach the same end, why spend more resources?

Arts and sports provide good opportunities in the world today. Sportsmen and women earn a far more comfortable living than most other career professionals. I am of the opinion that our curriculum should put more emphasis in these areas. Sports are an important part of human life in terms of physical and psychological stability, especially in this video game madness era. Video games have kept our children indoors, most of whom tend to be very inactive and hence at risk of obesity and diseases associated with lack of physical activities.

Although it is well known that sports are also essential in intellectual and moral uplifting, it is an area that Tanzania has largely ignored. Tanzanian history does not tell a very good story in the area of sports. Our sports, both professional and amateur, are full of irregularities both in administration and on the fields. Corruption has attacked this area unsparingly. We have read and heard of so many court cases about misconduct in our sports. Our sports club houses, especially for football, have been turned into battlefields, where contending factions engage in regular punch-ups and other forms of violence in attempts to determine who holds the clubs' purses. Meanwhile we have failed to produce any coherent sports development programs for our children in schools, our domestic experience has been a continuous disappointment and our international performance a disaster except on the very few occasions when individual talent, effort and determination have yielded the lone medal that we have seldom cheered.

In a nutshell our education has setbacks that need scrutiny. While the third government under Mkapa made commendable efforts in rehabilitating our schools' infrastructure in terms of buildings, desks, etc., more emphasis should be put on improving our schools in terms of quality of education in general. Our education policy needs to be redefined and our mission and objectives of education both elementary and advanced levels should be reviewed to see that they meet the demands of the new era.

Universities

Tanzania has recently embarked in a fashion of converting junior colleges into university colleges. That has increased the number of universities in the country, which in turn has had the effect of giving opportunities to more students who want to pursue their dreams to the highest levels of academia. Colleges such as Mzumbe University formerly the Institute of Development Management (IDM – Mzumbe), Sokoine University formerly University of Dar es Salaam faculty of Agriculture, Ardhi University formerly University College of Land and Surveying (UCLAS) the former ARDHI INSTITUTE; Muhimbili University College of Health Science formerly the faculty of health sciences of the University of Dar es Salaam; and other private colleges like Tumaini University; International Medical and Technological University (IMTU); University of Saint Augustine, formerly Nyegezi College; Hubert Kairuki Memorial University, Mount Meru University, formerly International Baptist Theological Seminary, were all recently upgraded to universities and many others are in the process.

Politically and socially we may take pride and hold it up as a sign of progress. But there is a technical question that seeks to know if this is really progress both academically and economically. Academically the question is whether all these universities do provide the desired quality of education.

An example here is the University Dar es Salaam (UDCM). This is one institution in which Tanzanians should have taken great pride. UDSM has a proud legacy as a historic institution of our country. It has made a great contribution to the development of our country through the number of professionals it has trained during the many years of its long existence. But it is sad to see how this important center of learning for the country is being run presently. Excellence should have been the defining attribute of this place where the cream of intellectuals stays, but instead mediocrity rules. I did not intend to go deep into specifics in this book; but I have found myself in some instances being forced to. The academic and cultural standards of UDSM are constantly deteriorating. Somebody somewhere must not be doing her job well. Studying at this college is not very different from surviving in a jungle – it is for the fittest, for you cannot stand all the strikes and protests if you are not physically fit. There are also many ways of making good grades without hard work. The quality of education is very poor in terms of facilities and methodology. Students complain about the number of students in classes for classes are uncontrollably oversized. This diminishes the expected intellectual intimacy between instructors and students. There are many other areas of complaints, e.g., meals, living conditions, accommodation, harassment, and of course corruption.

Our interviews, with students, concerning what they go through before they graduate from this college revealed more than we needed and more than we were capable of handling. Some of these revelations are too gross to be included in this book. In such conditions it is impossible to hope for the maintenance of the most basic standards in an institution of higher learning. My argument here is that more emphasis should be put on quality more than on the number of universities and other higher learning institutions.

Economically the problem lies in the fact that these colleges are being upgraded to universities without any replacement of the erstwhile junior colleges. No secondary school has been upgraded to a junior college; and the rate at which the junior colleges are established is very slow as compared to the rate of upgrade of the colleges to universities. Apparently we are creating a gap. These colleges were playing the very important role of preparing an intermediate work force, which, I believe is one of the most important links of the development of our economy construction, for we cannot have engineers without technicians. We cannot have doctors without medical assistants or nurses. We cannot have judges without court clerks. We cannot have chief accountants and auditors without cashiers.

If every college is transformed into a university, how are we going to prepare this necessary intermediate workforce? I think we should develop a tradition of treasuring these colleges and vocational schools. We need to maintain and keep them. Our biggest problem is work and production. My opinion is we should manage the changes, control the upgrading process and enhance quality.

A Cultural Challenge in Education
A craving for and the search for social admiration through college education has become the vogue in this nation. We are so deeply drowned in a culture that is exceedingly conscious of prestige that people go to extra lengths in search of the *"prestige"* of education credentials, even if it were fake ones. This brings in place the fact that in this culture it is not the professional skills or knowledge that matter. It's the prestige that counts. The multi-sectoral corruption virus, therefore, easily finds its way in the system, especially the college-level education system. No wonder we end-up with several *Doctors of Philosophy* who can't philosophize anything!

According to the Ministry of Education and Vocational Training (MoEVT) 2011 report, there are presently over thirty (30) public universities and eleven (11) private universities. This is perhaps a good step after 50 years of independence. But there is a critical concern about the products of these universities. It is much less the number of universities *(after, all we need more of them)* but the question is whether or not these universities provide the desired quality of education.

Our recent fashionable embanking on turning our junior colleges into universities speaks for itself about our obsession. Colleges were upgraded until the government intervened and placed some kind of censure to this glorious exercise. But accepting so much change within so short a time, chances are high that we will fail to manage and direct the changes, and fail to maintain the requisite standards. Sadly, this is already happening.

UDSM should have maintained a posture similar to that of Harvard or Yale and Cambridge or Oxford in the USA and UK respectively. These highly reputable colleges stand for nothing but quality and excellence. Graduates from these colleges are almost guaranteed well-paying careers, *almost anywhere in the world,* even before graduating. Unlike them, UDSM's reputation is diminishing with time.

A combination of rapid upgrade of colleges and the unquenched thirst for prestige supplemented by our inferior supervisory and regulatory authorities has mostly resulted in very mediocre products with only a few exceptions.

Tanzania is now replete with people with college degrees: BSc's, BA's, PGD's and MBA's as well as CPA's and PhD's. A good test of this achievement would be a proactive approach to the political, economic, scientific and technological problems of our country, in which case more research publications with tangible solutions to our local problems, *corresponding to the number of graduates*, would to be available; scientific and technological innovations increased; fine literary and scientific works be written; and more innovative ideas developed. On the contrary these credentials remain as just means to promote social status.

Instead of promoting brilliance and creativity, our colleges remain places to offer certificates without the said qualifications. Very little impact has been felt from our university graduates. This is because our college system doesn't prepare people to become independent thinkers, but more of becoming individuals who simply conform to prevailing ideas. Robert Fritz (1991), a composer, filmmaker and author, suggested that, "The creative process has had more impact, power, influence, and success than any other process in history. All of the arts, many of the sciences, architecture, pop culture, and the entire technological age we live in exists because of the creative process" (p. 5).

Because most of our colleges prepare people to be reactive instead of proactive to problem solving, little improvement is expected in managing and solving our economic and political problems. Gerard J Puccio, Ph.D. in his article, "Creative learning in our high education classroom," talks about a survey made in the USA back in 1990. He says, "In 1990 a study was published by the American Society for Training and Development. The main thrust of this nationwide investigation was to identify the skills deemed necessary in today's workplace. One of the seven basic skill sets identified by the research team was creative thinking and adaptability."

People with college degrees are the ones responsible for changing the country by their creative and intellectual input. These are people who should invent new ideas compatible to our ways of life and our values. These are the ones expected to offer solutions to our long-lasting economic and political problems. They are the people to develop the manufacturing sector and the public organizations that are perishing right in front of our eyes. But these people use credentials just as labels for gaining admiration and reputation. Too high a cost is subsequently channeled to an almost cultural infection of dependence on foreign professionals.

Employment
If there is a problem that has triggered the exodus of multitudes of Tanzanians to foreign lands, it is the issue of unemployment and underemployment. We have lost quite a bit of manpower as a

consequence of this problem. Everywhere in Europe and America, there are organized communities, quite large in numbers, of Tanzanians, some of whom are very good professionals that chose, for the very noble cause of their survival, to contribute to the development of other countries.

Under the second phase government the edifice on which the policy of socialism was built crumbled with the beginning of the denationalization of all the major means of production. This process reached its climax under the third phase government which completed the task of privatization, making sure that the quasi-totality of all means of production were put back into private hands. This was partly due to the harsh realities the country lived through under the failed implementation of Ujamaa, which did not answer the high aspirations of the people.

One area that was directly hard-hit as a result of radical privatization is employment. Up till the privatization exercise the employment scene looked quite comfortable with almost every university graduate guaranteed a job with the state sector, including Parastatal Organizations, the chief employer. From about 1991-92 the government ceased to be the chief employer. A few years later it started retrenching even those who it already had employed. This was one of the most damaging outcomes of uncontrolled privatization.

Today, more than 300 public and governmental organizations have proudly been privatized under the Parastatal Sector Reform Commission (PSRC). What this meant, in part, was that decisions as to employment shifted from the public sector into the private sector, whose main interest was, of course, maximization of profit, and the unemployment rate has been climbing ever since. Presently the market is flooded with unemployed professionals of all cadres. Job hunting has turned out to be a profession in itself fueled by the art of corruption and favoritism.

For a while, the buzzword in our economy system was "redundancy". There was redundancy everywhere; redundancy in the National Bank of Commerce (NBC); redundancy in the Tanzania Harbors Authority (THA); redundancy in central government; redundancy in the electricity company (TANESCO), redundancy in the telephone company (TTCL); in the railway company (TRC), redundancy in the shipping company (NASACO); redundancy in the insurance company (NIC); redundancy in the revenue authority (TRA); redundancy in the police force, redundancy anywhere and everywhere in the surviving public organizations . We saw redundancy on television, we heard redundancy on radios, and we read about redundancy in newspapers-redundancy,

redundancy everywhere-we actually dreamt about redundancy. By then we had already started forgetting about companies and organizations like Regional Trading Company (RTC), Small Industrial Development Organization (SIDO), General Agricultural Exports (GAPEX), and National Milling Corporation (NMC) which were either completely dead or in a coma after the radical changes of our economic system.

We were assaulted by redundancy. People's lives were made miserable by redundancy. It was a terrible time for, say, an employee in a parastatal organization to live in a constant fear of one day getting up and going to her workplace only to find out that her job was gone, just like that, a job she had had for years and on which she and her family solely depended. Some of the people swept aside by this tide will remember this word, "redundancy" to their dying day.

Although there has been so much bitterness and so many complaints concerning redundancy, it still may be pertinent to determine that redundancy was and is, in itself, not as horrific as we may desire to conclude. It was the poor implementation, with the attendant corruption, favoritism, nepotism, which produced so much that was objectionable. The timing and pacing may also have been impolitic, and lacked adequate preparation and information.

In the circumstances, the laying off of surplus labor could be defended on the ground that it was a necessary evil, especially in an era in which the mantra of privatization was a universal phenomenon. This is the new harsh reality of our world today. We have been told that in order to develop, we must privatize, and to privatize there must be efficiency and cost-effective production; hence redundancy, with all its fancy terminology of retrenchment, downsizing, and rightsizing comes in the picture.

Subsequently, we have a flooded market of unemployed and non-utilized professionals. Unemployment has grown at a terrifying pace. Unfortunately the study of the benefits of privatization did not include the study of the survival of these formerly poorly paid, now retrenched people. Many people are suffering out there, not because they are too dull to think for themselves but because the system has divorced them so brutally. No preparation was made for these people to encounter unemployment or adapt to self-employment. Most of the retrenched employees had not been brought up to employ themselves or to battle it out in the rough and tumble of a privatized job market. All they knew was: go to school, study hard, make good grades, and the government will assure you of a job, period. Now the latter part has sublimed – it is just going to school, making good grades, and coming to join others on the streets.

In his paper to the University of Dar es Salaam Convocation (2003) Idd Simba said (2003), "the single most significant political mistake we made in this country was to embark upon the rapid program of privatization, especially of the major and sensitive Parastatal, before the whole system was fully understood by stakeholders." Simba continues by saying, "Despite the admittedly poor performance of state enterprises and the rationale for the privatization program, there were far too many people whose livelihoods depended on state enterprises. African Tanzanians had developed a sense of ownership of their economy through the public sector… It should not at all be surprising that the Arusha de-nationalization of state assets is still causing turmoil in our community."

No exercise was carried out with such recrimination and ill-feeling as were the twin programs of privatization and retrenchment. Though the objectives and goals were clear to the leadership, still the approach and timing left much to be desired. The people who were adversely affected were not prepared. It is in light of this that there can be little justification for the self-congratulatory testimonies of the third phase government singing praises of the benefits of privatization. Most of the praises are one-sided in that they too conveniently neglect to point out the negative aspects of the program, but also, some of these benefits could have been achieved without such a brutal and heartless retrenchment, which has cost too many of our people in terms of taking away their very of livelihoods.

Labor Force
According to the 2002 estimates, Tanzania has a population of about 35 million people. According to the United Republic of Tanzania (URT) statistics, there was only a work force of 16,006,178 in 1999 with an increase of 3% per annum. This means that there was a total work force of 18.5 million in 2004. It is estimated that only 8.5% of these have had post-elementary training. 50% of this work force is estimated to be within the youth group bracket of 18 – 29 years of age. And more than 85% of all the labor force is in the rural and informal sectors that are characterized by low income, low value goods, and which are confined to the local market. It is only 6% of the total work force is in the formal sector. Unfortunately the informal sector is growing at an exponential rate, partly because of the migration from rural areas caused by increased unemployment in the rural areas and very limited formal sector employment. Taking the city of Dar es Salaam as an example, it had a population of about 250,000 people in 1965 but the number is more than ten times that today.

It is said that at present the employment in the formal public sector is almost stagnant. The formal private sector grows at a rate of 8 – 9% which is only about 10% of the new entrants to the labor market. 90% are left out! Lord have mercy!

This is clearly a big challenge our nation is facing. If we can manage to raise the number of school graduates, we should as well be concerned with the after-school life of these people. Mkapa's government played a very perplexing role of both emphasizing the increase of school-goers and minimizing employment opportunities!

Pension and Social Security

Among other things, retirement benefits and post-retirement social security have been real problems for many Tanzanians for a long time under National Provident Fund (NPF). The problem of insecurity after retirement has greatly contributed to foul plays and mischief in our economy. Many people have engaged in corruption and other dirty games to make sure that life does not turn into hell on them after they leave their offices. They have resorted to dirty tricks in order to stash away something to supplement the meager benefits they received. This is partly the cause of accumulation of illegal wealth that the third phase government tried to address but failed.

In 1975 NPF was re-organized into a Parastatal organization from a government framework (since 1964). Since July 1998 it has been known as National Social Security Fund (NSSF). In 1978 Parastatal Pension Fund (PPF) was established as a department of the National Insurance Corporation. In 1992, PPF was made an independent entity. Now we have Public Service Pension Fund (PSPF) and Local Authority Pension Fund (LAPF). Improvement has been made in these organizations. There are just impressive reports on the growth of NSSF, PSPF and PPF in terms of the membership (with NSSF leading with membership of more than 400,000), contributions, and investment projects. These organizations are getting stronger financially every day. The question on the other hand, is whether they provide a satisfying financial security to Tanzanians after their service to the nation. This is in terms of follow-ups of the benefits and the amount that retirees get.

There have been concerns that some of these pension funds have transformed themselves into real estate companies concentrating more on construction projects and making profits while neglecting the primary objectives for the stakeholders. This is a shift of objectives and needs to be looked into.

Retirement is thus a scary prospect in Tanzania. People lie about their age in order to remain in office; others have wished death would attend them in their office chairs rather than facing Tanzanian retirement life. That is how scary retirement in Tanzania has become. We need to work out something. We need to give our forerunners the life they deserve after their honorable service to the nation. If someone can faithfully give 20, 30, 40, 50 or 60 years to the nation through service and payroll taxes, they deserve much better. And we urge the responsible parties to do nothing but better.

Utilities
Water
Water (the lack of) and pollution are said to be the two greatest future global threats. Increased population and the attendant abuse of natural resources are deemed to be the causes of these foreseen threats.

Tanzania has been struggling with the issue of water for ages, and up until now we have not succeeded in providing clean and safe water for our people. These threats, which have a global dimension, are likely to be more menacing in countries such as ours because of the failure to put in place adequate mechanisms for the progressive provision of quality social services since 1961, when Tanganyika acquired her independence.

Although as far back as 1971 the government declared its intent of providing clean water to all Tanzanians by 2002. Today, more than 30 years after, the plan is still a pipedream. A major project is underway to provide water to Mwanza, Shinyanga, and Tabora from Lake Victoria, but we are yet to know its completion target and how much service this project is intending to offer. I have not quite resolved the puzzle of why a country like Tanzania with water almost everywhere could still go thirsty.

As with most social services, residents in urban areas fare a little better as compared to those living in rural areas. Statistics indicate that more than 45% of the people in rural areas do not have access to clean water. Shinyanga, Singida, Dodoma, Tabora, Arusha, Mwanza, Lindi, Coast, Kilimanjaro, Mara and Mtwara are said to be in greater need than other regions. Women in the rural areas of these regions spend five to twenty hours a week fetching water. This equals a good portion of a part-time job. These women walk five to ten km to the water sources. This is terrible! In absolute numbers only 14,553,853 Tanzanians were getting clean water by 2004. That is only slightly higher than 41% of the entire Tanzanian population. More than 58% of the people are in serious trouble as far as water is concerned. Now I am not suggesting that we have not made progress in this important social service; in comparison with 1971 when we could provide water to only 1.4 million people it indicates that there has been some progress. But we had an opportunity to do better than that by far during the past fifty-year period, and nor should we forget that our population has grown exponentially.

Residents of Dar es Salaam still experience trouble every now and then because of rainfall and the old age of distribution pipes from Ruvu. They break so frequently, therefore there is often times a shortage of water. One straight forward approach to this problem is rehabilitation and modernization of the water distribution systems. We at least can afford this on our own. We need to make sure the little we have and can afford is in its best state of operation by providing steady, regular and periodic maintenance. This will increase reliability and dependability, hence reduce major repair costs caused by major break downs. In addition we also need to deal very severely with recklessness, negligence, or sabotage of any kind. It is shocking to know that many of our problems are caused by carelessness and leniency in dealing with irresponsible parties. This has affected not only the water sector, but many other areas of our economy. Law enforcement and accountability need to be greatly enhanced.

Electricity
Tanzania Electric Supply Company Limited (TANESCO) is the sole distributer of electricity in the country. TANESCO generates, transmits, distributes and sells electricity. The government took full ownership of the company in 1975 when the government showed interest between 1964 and '75 to buy shares of the previously owned private power companies, Former Tanganyika National Electric Supplies Company (TANESCO) established on 26th November 1931; and Former Dar es Salaam and District Electric Supply Company Ltd (DARESCO). TANESCO sells power to individual customers on the mainland as well as bulk power to Zanzibar Electricity Corporation (ZECO), which in turn sells to its customers in the islands of Zanzibar. (Source: www.tanesco.co.tz)

TANESCO's generation system consists of hydro, coal, thermal and gas. According to TANESCO website, Between October 2009 to September 2010, Hydro power constitutes 73% of all power generation. The rest was Gas and Thermo. This is mainly from the hydro-electricity stations at *Mtera* (80 MW), *Kihansi* (180 MW), *Kidatu* (204 MW) *New Pangani Falls* (68 MW), Hale (21 MW) and *Nyumba ya Mungu*, in Moshi, Kilimanjaro (2 MW). Sources of electro-power from Songo Songo natural gas are TANESCO Ubungo (100 MW), TANESCO Tegeta (45 MW), Songas (180 MW) and Symbion Power (75 MW). Power generated from crude oil is MW 100 MW from IPTL at Tegeta, Dar es Salaam.. Kidatu has been the major source with about 50% of the normal 561 MW of power supply by TANESCO.

However, electricity is still awfully insufficient in Tanzania. TANESCO has only managed to reach less than 20% customers among the Tanzanian people, currently estimated to be 40m. To be exact, according to the Mwananchi Newspaper, of January 12th, 2011, despite TANESCO's long history of over 100 years of existence, it only serves 17% of the Tanzanian population, 15% of which are urban customers.

Getting electricity in turns has been the norm for many years. Between the months of January and June, 2006 electrical supply was a nightmare. April and October 2011 was worse. Some of the electric power sources were closed due to lower levels of water and people continued to share insufficient electricity by distributing the scarce power. Rationing dropped from getting electricity 16 hrs a day to 12 hrs and even less.

Meanwhile TANESCO has been blamed for many problems: poor and old infrastructure; failure to collect debts from mega-customers; poor power production and distribution; and the high tariffs charged by the company despite the prevailing problems. Many people accused the government's hand in TANESCO for the interest of few people who were said to want TANESCO dead for their interests. The situation of the company was probably worse during the third phase government during which many companies with interest in power production and distribution were registered, some as mentioned before, closely associated with the President himself.

The dark clouds kept hovering over the ministry of Energy and Minerals. Issues of *fuel and electricity* started an unprecedented discussion in the parliament with a subsequent scandal of the Permanent Secretary (PS) soliciting funds from institutions under the ministry on what was termed as facilitating the budget to have the annual budget sail through with minimum opposition. The fact of the matter was: the Minister for Energy and Mineral was in a difficult position to convince the parliament to pass the budget because it was coincidentally at the time with the worst power rationing. Meanwhile chaos and strikes in the sale of petrol fuel were prevailing countrywide.

The PS was sent on a paid leave for a month. He was, thereafter cleared by the CAG's – *Controller and Auditor General's* - and reported to have had no misconduct whatsoever. The Chief Principal Secretary instructed the PS to resume work with immediate effect. The parliament started a motion to stop discussing 2011/12 budget as from then until the CAG's report was to be brought to the parliament.

After strange twists and turns of this issue the President intervened and instructed the PS to continue with his leave with unspecified limit of time. A parliamentary committee was formed on Nov. 2011 under the chairmanship of Eng. Ramo M. Makani to probe the matter. Gross irregularities were later revealed and the PS, CAG and CS were implicated in the scandal.

This, like the water problem, is also fueled by recklessness and unaccountability. The scandals we have heard recently defeat our efforts towards improving power supply.

The most irksome aspect of TANESCO's saga is the unreliability and unpredictability of power supply. Power can go off at any time for any reason and for any length of time. In the 21st century, at a time when the technological world seems to know no bounds, and when dizzying inventions are being revealed on a daily basis, Tanzanians are still struggling with an unreliable power supply. How can this ever help us survive in this world of competition?

The electrical power supply has proven completely inadequate for our needs. It is inadequate in volume and unreliable in its distribution. This has impacted most negatively on our industries, many of which have collapsed because of the short supply and unreliability of our electricity, not to mention the high tariffs of electricity in Tanzania compared to the other members of the East African Community. At a time when we are trying hard to attract foreign investment it is imperative to look into the electrical power problem with new seriousness, knowing that potential investors consider electric power as guaranteed for their productive purposes as well as an essential utility. I remember reading a story back in 2003 by a columnist in University of Alabama at Birmingham's paper (UAB), Kaleidoscope, in which the columnist was suggesting that the world was approaching its end. Her reasons were, she claimed, the existence of obvious signs. She gave a number of signs; and one of the signs was the five day power blackout in New York in August 2003. To her, the 5-day power blackout was not something within the norm; and she represents many people from the developed world that come to our country for investment opportunities.

The disappointing story is that Tanzania has a higher potential for natural energy than most other countries in this world. There are so many natural sources of energy in our country that have remained untapped for all these years. We are told that many energy sources remain underdeveloped because of poor technology and lack of capital. That does not seem very convincing. If we have energy, we can make money out of it; therefore it is important that we develop plans that can facilitate production of this energy.

Safety and Security
This is another crucial area that needs enhancement in its entire framework, mode of operation and implementation. The situation is now scary. Measures are to be taken before it gets worse and spins completely out of control. What we need are especially improvement in the use of technology, and accountability.

Tanzanians for most of the country still live very vulnerable and insecure lives. At homes, in travels, at the banks, in business, in downtown streets and in the countryside, Tanzanian life has become extraordinarily risky. Dar es Salaam and Arusha have been recorded with scary levels of crimes lately. In the years 2002, 2003 and 2004 numerous daylight robberies were recorded, and though a few were thwarted, many succeeded. In some of these robberies and attempted robberies many lives were lost and huge amounts of money stolen. There was, for instance, the case of CRDB Bank losing millions of US Dollars in Dar es Salaam in July 2002 and the other one in May 2004 when the National Bank of Commerce, in Moshi, Kilimanjaro, also lost huge sums in what was said to be the worst heist ever in the history of armed robbery in Tanzania. Many other high-scale robberies occurred before these, such as that of Simbaulanga who vanished with millions of NBC money in the late 1980s.

Other branches that were burglarized in recent years, according to the report by the Director of Criminal Investigations were: Postal Bank Arusha Branch, Exim Bank Mtwara branch and NMB Igunga branch in Tabora and many other bureaux de change.

The year 2006 did not start any better. Many banks were robbed in Dar es Salaam in the first four months of 2006. Bravo to police forces where they rescued millions of tax-payers' money and where they managed to counterattack theft and robbery plans. But it is of no doubt that security is increasingly becoming a challenge to our forces.

Crimes range from on-street robberies, to car thefts, and even theft at accident scenes where the severely injured or the dead bodies are robbed of their belongings! This is pathetic. It is an inhumanity of the highest order.

We have even heard warnings in commuter buses and in trains in Dar, Ausha, Isevya - Tabora, and Itigi – Singida, etc., saying something like, "We are now approaching the zone of thugs and robbers; take off all your valuable ornaments: watches, rings, necklaces, earrings, and any gold looking items and stay away from the windows." I hate this alert and every time I have been among the passengers in such situations I have felt like surrendering a greater measure of my freedom in my own free land where peace is believed to belong. It is as if we are satisfied with our role as victims. Everybody knows where criminals are and yet nothing is done to deal with the situation.

Then we have the numerous and irksome thefts and pilferages that take place in our ports, which cater not only for goods destined for Tanzania, but also goods in transit to our neighbors, the landlocked countries of Uganda, Rwanda, Burundi, DR Congo, Zambia and Malawi. Because of the importance of this traffic to these countries, our ports are significant foreign exchange earners, but their activities have been badly hampered and their reputation tarnished by acts of pilferage, involving every kind of item, from the smallest trinket to the largest container sizes. It is very disturbing to realize how much money we have lost because of safety issues in our ports.

It must be realized, however, that improvement has been registered due to concerted efforts by the port authorities and the relevant government departments. The theft issues in our ports recently are considerably lower compared to those we heard about in the 1980s and 1990s of containers perishing from the Dar port every now and then. But there is still more to be done.

There are theft issues of all magnitudes in other important areas our societies too. Many areas are being haunted by lack of security: electrical cables cut for ornament, oil in our pipelines intercepted and siphoned out, and buses on roads waylaid by bandits, etc. There is no doubt then, that we need to come up with significantly improved countermeasures to confront this grave security problem. The advancement of technology and illegal possession of guns have increased the incidences of organized crimes. The result is that the nation's security has been compromised as never before. To make matters worse, more and more people can now possess guns legally. This has compounded the problem. Technically, the problem here is not those who rightfully possess weapons, but after liberalization of gun ownership even those who possessed the guns illegally before, have found it more convenient to use theirs. It is dangerous!

I may not necessarily be against the liberalization of gun ownership, but my opinion is that we needed more preparation of modern control schemes before allowing it and leaving everything to individuals. While we are very proud of our old-fashioned police force, it's time to realize now that change happens very fast in every area of life including crime and theft. The fight against these crimes should be of matching intensity. We need law enforcement agencies that are technologically savvy.

Theft in corporate organizations and government ministries turned out to be the norm in the last two decades. The very people entrusted by the public with the safeguard and protection of the resources of our country decided to abuse the trust. Forgeries, corruption, and many unprofessional conducts were the protocols of daily activities in the government offices, embassies and corporate offices.

It's not too late yet, but the government should be more resolute on these issues. The prevailing situation may worsen in the near future, from the look of things. It is the duty of the government and of course the public to come up with improved and advanced systems of security. For we have to understand that when criminals see our hungry men and women in uniform walking around with clubs begging for a few shillings for their lunch, they feel like they can do anything, harm anybody and get into any office, including police stations, and take what they want. They feel like they own everything in the country. That is why some criminals and corrupt people gain social admiration. My advice to the fourth phase government is to prioritize security. Although this may not seem like a priority to some of us, it does impact our economy negatively. Things are now fueled by globalization and the free movement of people, ideas, and goods across the globe. The ease with which information can be accessed and manipulated and the possibility of criminal conspiracy are high and important matters affecting our security. There are no firewalls of information between different sources locally and internationally, therefore there is much freedom of accessibility to and passing of information. This increases security risks.

National Identification System

An accurate, simple, and credible way of national identification is important during this era when technology and crime advance side by side. It is important to have a proper and modern mechanism of identifying and tracking people. I have heard of plans to have national identity cards before, but I have never seen any such card and have no clue as to what happened with the plans. Every person has a different form of identification in Tanzania, and a great portion of the population has no identification at all. This makes some tasks, e.g., prevention of crimes (robbery, fraud, corruption, murder, etc.), extremely complicated. Even otherwise benign undertakings, such as census or elections, are rendered extremely difficult by the lack of a proper identification system. While procedures may be underway to have national identity cards, more emphasis will serve an important task here. Proper identification schemes will enhance the country's security a great deal, and probably reduce costs in population estimates and elections. Just a simple form of identification is necessary.

Simplicity is important for one good reason. It conforms to the international security and legal standards. PI (Privacy International), an international organization for protection of personal privacy for

Northern and Latin American, European, and Asian countries suggests the importance of simple ID cards. It reads, "The higher the "integrity" (infallibility) of a card, the greater is its value to criminals and illegal immigrants. A high-value card attracts substantially larger investment in corruption and counterfeit activity. The equation is simple: higher value ID equals greater criminal activities." So we need a simple form of identity card that will help the police and intelligence departments in their undertakings without necessarily attracting the investment of high-stake criminal players.

The use of modern technology for record keeping with computer software should be utilized as a prop for the identification scheme. A national-wide database for identification and record keeping should be established. Without posing any threat to the privacy of personal information, proper records and data should be kept confidential at the same time made readily accessible for use and reference whenever required by the authorities.

I was asked a question during one of my interviews in the preparation of this book: why do I think we need a formal identification system, to which I replied simply that because there are many evils being perpetrated under concealed identities. The death of a young lady in a hotel in Arusha whose identity and the killer's were never known in September 2003 was a perfect example. I am fully convinced that identification schemes are an important aspect of security enhancement.

4

Economy

Economic Goals

While attending school in the USA, in one of my class projects, I happened to participate in what was known as the X-prize competition. This was a competition for promoting private aircraft tours in outer space. Until that time space shuttles were organized exclusively under US government sponsorship. At this point in time a group of engineers thought that it was time for another step of technological advancement. They set out to develop a private space vehicle for individuals who wanted to experience what it feels like to be out of this world. If this mission proved successful, which it did, a winner would receive a cash reward of US $10 m - about ten billion Tanzanian shillings (Tshs. 10B), by the exchange rates then. This was definitely an idea that would potentially revolutionize conventional tourism in a very radical way. Those fed up with repetitive visits to other earthly attractions would now have something better to aim at.

I liked this project very much because of the challenge it posed to me as a student and as a poor third world country citizen; so I invested a considerable amount of my time in it. I was particularly keen with what other people do in attempts to improve and advance technology. I also wanted to learn more about it; I therefore followed it up until the end when a winner was declared. In the process I learnt about who was behind it all. It was a very young lady who co-sponsored this project. She, in fact, gave the greater part of sponsorship of this competition. This was none other than Anousheh Ansari, a brilliant scientist with an interesting success story behind.

Anousheh Ansari's story began back in Iran. As a naturalized American citizen, Ansari moved to America at the age of 16, where she pursued a career in computer engineering. After graduation, she worked for private companies, but realized soon that she would exploit her talents better in her own private practice. With a blending of intelligence, hard work and a good economic environment she started her own company in Telecommunications in the spring of 1993. Eight years latter, when she was in her 30's, her company was worth US $600 million (Tshs. 600 billion). It was this huge success in her business venture coming in less than a decade that made Ansari one of the most successful electrical and computer engineers the world has ever known.

However, Ansari is not a very isolated case. There are a number of other business people in computer engineering and other professions in the USA who had more-or-less similar stories. Dikembe Mutombo Mpolondo Mukamba Jean Jacques Mutombo is originally from Congo.

In 1987, at the age of 22 years he went to America for studies. Gifted also in sports and humanitarian activities, a basketball coach diverted Mutombo's dream into professional basketball as he was pursuing his pre-med to become an MD. As of today Mutombo has graduated with a double major in linguistics and diplomacy. He is said to be fluent in four international languages and five local dialects. Mutombo has received hundreds of awards and honors for helping the fight against diseases in Africa. He travels all around Africa during his off-seasons. Above all Mutombo rewarded his country, the Democratic Republic of Congo, with a 300-bed modern hospital at a 29-million US $ cost (more than Tshs. 29 Billion) in Kinshasa, among which he personally contributed US $18.5 million. The hospital is named after his mother, Biamba Marie Mutombo. This is another son of Africa whose life says one thing loudly: that all he missed was a good environment.

These are results of a dynamic economy. Many people in America make changes in their lives within a short time. We know of people like Bill Gates, Michael Dell, Alice Walton, Larry Page, Oprah Winfrey and many others who are said to have had, among other things, as reasons for their success, the best economic environment in which to operate. This would only be possible in a very flexible and rewarding economic atmosphere. Ansari and Mutombo made such remarkable contributions to the development of technology and health because they benefited from a very rewarding economic system. Now, this is not a call for "coming to America" to African youth. It is rather a challenge ahead of us to make our country a place where the rest of the world would love to come to work.

USA is one of the greatest economies in the world because of two cardinal reasons, its flexibility and dynamism. The American economy is blind to citizenship, bureaucracy and nepotism. Entrepreneurs are certainly encouraged by such an environment. The Government is very supportive, the infrastructure is excellent and overall the microeconomic policies are less bureaucratic and very supportive of business starters. This is the kind of economy that brings development.

Unlike the American economy, another economic giant, the United Kingdom is generally believed to have a very rigid economy despite both being characterized as Anglo-Saxon economies. It is not as easy to make changes in the UK within one lifetime. There are two distinct economic categories of people in the UK, the poor and the rich; and in either case, the trend continues down the generations. Mostly, wealth is inheritable in UK and that's why UK is said to have the highest poverty rate among large economies. It is not very easy for one person from the poor class to move up the social ladder and enter a new economic class. It is especially more difficult for a foreigner.

UK is very different from URT. The living standards are very different. The lower class in the UK is a lot better off compared to her Tanzanian counterpart; this calls us to action if we are to compare even remotely with these economies. As an ultimate goal we need to raise the lower end of our life standard. The gap that has developed in recent years between the lower and upper classes among people of the same stream of life should be considerably reduced.

Tanzanians need a flexible and dynamic economy, an economy that gives equal chance of success to all of the citizens regardless of their social status, race, or family background, an economy that rewards hard work and initiative – an economy that encourages people to work hard and ethically in pursuit of success; and an economy that gives people the opportunity to contribute to other sectors of life because they have benefited from a good economic atmosphere and have trust in the leadership of their nation.

Such an economy is evident by the constantly raising living standards of the citizens. It is obvious that such an economy cannot be the type that is shallow, with limited and unreachable opportunities, a rigid economy that is for some chosen, fortunate few, especially when our standards are so low.

It should be clear to most observers that over the recent years it has not been easy for most of our people to make any headway in economic terms, to the extent that unless one is willing and able to engage in shady deals success remains in an indefinite hold and it is next to a miracle. The policies and laws in place for small business have become a "glass ceiling"- if I may borrow this phrase– to small businessmen. Bureaucratic policies need to be checked out. A very significant reminder is the fact that the third phase government retrenched millions of people who initially depended fully on employment. These people need back their lives. But because the government may not be able to get them back, their livelihood then should be through other channels of economy. Self-employment and entrepreneurship policies should be flexible and dynamic enough to help these people. Corruption in the entire economic and social system should be brought to a halt.

The Tanzanian economic experience is indeed unique. The duration of the transitional period to move from one level to the other seems to be infinite. The promises of a better life have remained unfulfilled. The hardships of life have persisted even more and people's lamentations are heard everywhere because of the mismanagement and underutilization of our resources. A new promise by the 4th phase administration of a living wage to its employees has remained but rhetoric.

At the time of great trouble, during, and immediately after the Kagera war, Tanzanians were called upon to tighten their belts for a short period of time, one-and-a-half years, after which the economy could improve. The sad thing was, the hard times went on and on for so long that the people lost all hope. Actually the economy increasingly worsened ever since. The re-construction of our economy since the war has remained undone – an impossible mission.

In recent years Tanzanians have been told over and over again that the economy of their country has grown impressively. Their hope is one day to practically feel the improvement which has so far remained in official statistics only. It is very ironic to say that for all this time this has remained a paper statistic only. Most Tanzanians are still suffering a great deal. At the beginning of the third phase government Tanzanians were told another short story: that our economy would not improve overnight. It would take a couple of years before they would actually feel the changes. Years and decades are passing by without much hope of change. The improvement of the Tanzanian economy is a theoretical myth that immeasurably defeats the comprehension of a peasant in Mkomaindo – Masasi; it does not have any impact on the real lives of the people yet. The third phase government has been very "smart" in using data and statistics to prove how marvelous it has performed economically during its ten-year tenure. Reality betrays them.

One does not need to be a rocket scientist to feel the fruits of a good economy, and as a lay-person in economics, I would assume that economic improvement would be evidenced practically by better lives - better social services, balanced development between urban and rural areas, security of citizens, empowerment of women, better wages and income, more employment opportunities, better nutrition, less disease, longer life expectancy of people and in our case, improved agriculture. It is a pity to note that most of the criteria above are still far reaching, while most of them should have been achieved at least to some extent if our rulers had been a little more focused on the job at hand. Theories put out by the Mkapa government suggest that our economy has probably reached the highest growth rate ever; but a present typical Tanzanian life is probably the most difficult experience ever since independence.

Industry

Industrial development has been one of the biggest challenges to all phases of the administration of our country. Since the 1970s the manufacturing sector has been going down steadily. The period from 1980 to 1984 is said to have been the worst time in the history of Tanzanian de-industrialization when our manufacturing sector recorded a decline at an annual average rate of 5%. A temporary relief of industrial growth at a rate of 2.3% followed between the years 1985 to 1989 but later the contribution of the same to the country's GDP dropped from 10.2 % to 8% between the years 1990 and 1994 nearing the gross domestic product of 1967 when we were only capable of simple manufacturing and processing of primary commodities.

The two biggest problems of the industrial sector are infrastructure and the habit we have developed of giving preference to trading over manufacturing. Many other problems have been said to cause the traumatic fall of our industries. These include lack of foreign exchange, working capital, and technological capability. The combination of these factors is said to have formed a very complicated situation in not only industrial productivity but even in the quantifying and studying of our manufacturing sector.

With achievement of independence, our nation, just like many other African states was determined to improve its economy. Following the world's industrial liberation, our countries wanted to replace the traditional agricultural economy by an industrial economy. This was meant to enhance production from small scale manufacturing to production of capital goods and goods to be used in the production of other goods.

Therefore industrial development was an important agenda in the early days of our nation. Latin America had done well with ISI (Import Substitution Industrialization). African states wanted to take the same route, but it did not seem to be a good option for this region of the world.

Following the failure of ISI, our country was forced to adopt the SAPs (Structural Adjustment Programs) in the eighties. This was probably a better option, but numerous factors were attributed to economic growth and therefore there were still many errors to be corrected. Actually researchers suggest that SAPs also have not brought the anticipated improvement. Although SAPs were touted as the answer to our economic problems, in Tanzania as elsewhere in Africa, they eventually proved a massive failure because they were predicated on wrong notions of the state abdicating its responsibilities in the provision of certain social goods, such as education and health, areas that the Breton woods institutions considered to be "unproductive." It was soon to be realized that there was no way a poor country like Tanzania was going to pull itself out of the trap of poverty if poor peasants could not send their children to school or get them treated when they fell ill. It is not for nothing that the SAPs have universally been recognized as the single most important factor that contributed to the 1980s being dubbed, "The Lost Decade."

To this day unreliability of electric power remains, among others, an aspect more closely associated with the challenges and downfall of industrial development of our country. So when we talk of manufacturing and industrialization generally we cannot avoid going back to the issue of those utilities, such as electric power and water supply, which are so crucial to industrial production and yet remain to this day most inaccessible in Tanzania. The state-owned utility companies seem to have failed, but even the efforts of the third phase government to lease these utilities to foreign companies have so far proved futile. Apart from the issue of accessibility and reliability, power tariffs per unit are highest in Tanzania compared to the other East African countries, and this has constituted a major disincentive for potential outside investors. In production, power and water are indispensable. But power and water in Tanzania are among the rarest commodities in terms of sufficiency and reliability.

The unfair competition imposed between our locally manufactured goods and imported goods has also had a hand in this. In the 1980s matters got completely out of hand following a laissez-faire liberalization of imports, without any form of limitation and without the necessary taxes, so that at some point imported goods seemed cheaper and better in quality. Apart from killing off the initiative of our own industry this situation created serious balance of payment problems for the country. Some commentators have suggested that the problem here is actually disguised. They believe that we over-protected our industries during the dominance of Ujamaa; hence they could not stand the wrath of competition after liberation.

A few industries have, today, become more productive than they were in the past, but their performance is still a far cry from what would be desired. It is quite deficient when compared to the desired development and advancement. Some industries, such as the machine-tools and agricultural-implements are all but dead.

But the third phase government has proudly proclaimed success in the area of beer industry, cigarette industry, sugar industry, wheat flour, etc. They believe strongly that more privatization would mean more success, although that is hard to justify considering the measure of irregularities that have been involved in the whole exercise. However, they truly deserve a credit at least for heading in the right direction.

Some industries which were moribund have been brought back to life under the recent policy reforms. These include Mgololo Paper Industries and Morogoro Polytex. New industries have also been established. These are Mwamba Breweries (Mbeya) TANWAT for timber exports, the cigarette industry (Iringa), waste plastic recycling industries and steel industry (Morogoro), etc. These have been established in the past two decades.

But many more have gone to the grave. We could cite the coffee, tea, cashew, beef and milk processing factories, and others that were doing well but are now nowhere to be seen. Probably the most conspicuous was the textiles industry that utilized our own local raw materials, especially cotton, but which underwent a dramatic decline in the 1980s and is now almost completely gone. The desolate ruins of what used to be Sunguratex and Kilitex, at Ukonga, on the outskirts of Dar es Salaam are testimony to this industrial decay, which has also negatively impacted on Tanzania's cotton, coffee and tobacco farmers.

Agriculture
Our agriculture has probably caused more debate and academic commentaries than anything else connected to third world economy. The debate may have been occasioned, partially, by a genuine scientific quest to get to the root of the problems of Tanzania's economic development and, partially, by an ideological tug-of-war between the protagonists in the battlefield of political philosophies between the contending currents of capitalism and socialism, each trying to score political points from what the Tanzanian leadership may or may not have done both pre- and post-Arusha declaration. The latter tries to place blame on everything else but the policy; and the former wants to point a finger at the socialist policy. The food crisis in 1974/75 attracted much international and local attention. According to UN reports, we had probably one of the highest domestic food production rates (7%) in the first decade after independence compared to our neighbors Kenya (5%). But after 1974 through the 1980s, the situation deteriorated dramatically. We were then one of the largest African recipients of food aid and in the 1980s we were in the balance of payment crisis.

According to our (Tanzanian) national website, "Agriculture in Tanzania is dominated by smallholder farmers (peasants) cultivating an average farm size of between 0.9 hectares and 3.0 hectares each. About 70 percent of Tanzania's crop area is cultivated by hand hoe, 20 percent by ox plough and 10 percent by tractor. It is rainfed agriculture. Food crop production dominates the agriculture economy and 5.1 million ha. are cultivated annually, of which 85 percent is for food crops. Women constitute the main part of the agricultural labor force. The major constraint facing the agriculture sector is the falling labor and land productivity due to application of poor technology, and the dependence on unreliable and irregular weather conditions. Both crops and livestock are adversely affected by periodical droughts." From here we may attempt to find out reasons for the absence of serious investment (local and international) in our agriculture.

Table 3: Agriculture's Contribution to the GDP

Year	% Contribution
1987	48.7
1988	47.6
1989	48.3
1990	47.9
1991	48.3
1992	48.0
1993	49.3
1994	49.6
1995	50.7
1996	50.6
1997	50.1
1998	49.1
1999	48.9
2000	48.2
2001	48.0

Source: http://www.tanzania.go.tz/agriculture.html.

As stated earlier on, agriculture has been the "backbone" (mainstay) of our economy, meaning that our economy has very high dependency on agriculture. This is true for these reasons: one, it is the major employing sector of the rural Tanzanian population which is 80% of all the Tanzanian population. Two, the contribution of this sector to the total GDP is higher than any other sector, and three, it is the main source of our foreign exchange because it has the highest contribution in exports. Agriculture constitutes 56% of the total present export volume of our country. Below is the table of the agriculture's contribution to the overall GDP between 1987 and 2001.

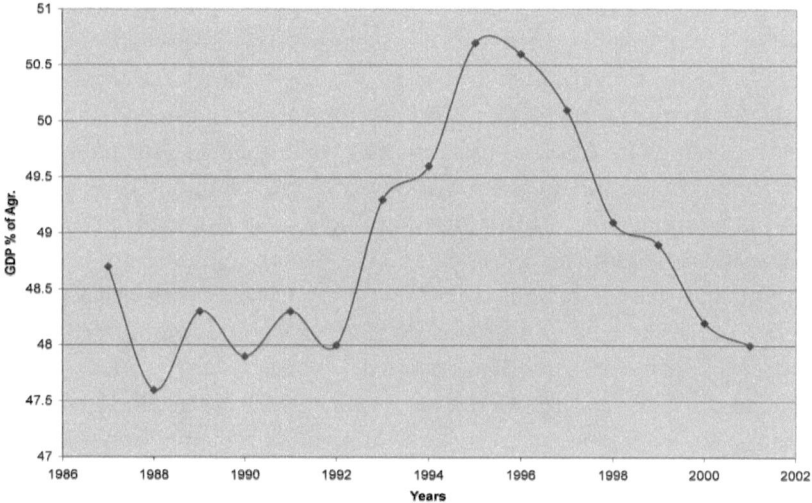

Fig. 5 Agriculture contribution to overall GDP between 1987 and 2001

Source: http://www.tanzania.go.tz/agriculture.html.

Table 3, which corresponds to Fig. 5 depicts the contribution of agriculture to the overall GDP. It is consistently showing about 49% average contributions over the 15 years which have been sampled.

Although agriculture was prioritized under the first phase government under Nyerere, there was not sufficient development.

In fact we witnessed a decline in the 1980s at rocket speed. The second and third phase governments have not placed enough emphasis on agriculture despite the ritual pronouncements of the importance of agriculture in the development of the economy. The third phase has been a "hero" in attracting foreign investors in other economic sectors like mining, telecommunications, banking, hotel, industry, tourism, etc., but has done very little in agriculture. My view is that if the Mkapa government had deployed as much effort in favor of agriculture as it did over in these other areas we would have witnessed improvements in all the other sectors because of the multiplier effect that agriculture would have had all round.

However, agriculture continued to be the biggest challenge of Mkapa's government to the end. In the 2003/04 budget session the Minister for Agriculture was quoted as saying that our agriculture had to clock a growth rate of more than 10% for it to stimulate any change in the economy. Recent statistics indicate that only 4.9% growth in agriculture had been recorded in 2004 and the average growth between 1987 and 2001 as recorded by the URT was 3.33% – far way from the declared goal.

In real terms this means that agriculture has almost remained stagnant. It is estimated (URT 2001a) that about 44 million ha. of Tanzanian land is agriculture friendly (arable), but only 23% (24.9 million acres) of this land is being utilized. This is representing a drop from the 29 million acres that were cultivated in 1964 and close to 39 million acres in 1970. There is no miracle here; it is just not going to work with this level of under-utility. 80% of Tanzanians depend on agriculture; nevertheless the growth is much lower than required. This represents serious under-utilization of the one resource that is essential to the livelihood of the majority of Tanzanians. Unless we resolve this problem we should not expect any miracle to happen and pull our people from their poverty and underdevelopment. At this point, it is not difficult to realize that four major problems have failed our agriculture.

Poor Infrastructure

Despite the efforts made by the Ministry of Works to improve our roads, for a long time our road network has been a great hindrance to our economic development. Many rural areas, rich in agricultural potential, are poorly served by our road network or are almost totally isolated. We have just seen through statistics that most rural roads (90%) are impassable during rain seasons and therefore have very limited or no access at all. There are high hopes that, with the current efforts, this may be a short term problem. However, it is true that we have gone on for five decades without a most vital infrastructure. A lot remains to be done in order to encourage those, local or foreign investors, who may want to invest in agriculture but are discouraged by the poor road network. Actually road construction and rehabilitation should have been emphasized in rural areas first.

Communication is also an issue. Tanzania has advanced very rapidly in the use of wireless telephony, which has grown exponentially over the past decade or so. But it is not reliable enough for big investors to rely on unless it is improved and made available to the remotest areas of the rural countryside. It seems therefore that the traditional land-line technology is still of great importance, and may have to be spread across the country to give a boost to agriculture-related communication.

Government Subsidy in Agriculture
Our government has refrained from subsidizing agriculture, and the agriculture budgetary allocation for the past four financial years averages about 4.7%. Now I am not sure if this will improve our economy which is heavily dependent on unsubsidized agriculture. Worse still, the farmers in Tanzania have no access to bank credits. According to current statistics by the World Bank, commercial bank lending for agriculture has halved in the past decade despite a tremendous increase in the number of commercial banks on the ground. In 1996 there was total domestic lending of 12% and the same was 6% in 2001. Except for Akiba Commercial Bank that seems to have a microfinance policy, most banks practice macro-finance and consider it a high risk lending to farmers and other small income people.

Poor Technology
Today, in the 21st century, only 0.2% of rural households in Tanzania own tractors. It is a scary thought that in this century, Tanzanians want to build their economy with a hand hoe and prayers for adequate rainfalls. And yet President Mkapa was at some stage talking about entering the 21st century majestically! For sure this is very majestic.

According to the District Integrated Agricultural Survey (1998/99) as quoted by Evelyne Lazaro and Ntengua Mdoe in their paper about the agriculture sector at the Convocation in 2003, only 35% of the farmers used fertilizers. 65% did not. After harvest only 57% of them used crop protection against pests in storage. Among these 34% used cow dung and leaves because they could not afford chemicals. Irrigation is another issue affecting our agriculture. In 2002 there was a shortage of rain and we were facing a great shortage of food. All the Minister for Agriculture did was thank God for bringing rain because otherwise the story would have been worse because of lack of any exit strategy from the situation. Notwithstanding our good faith in God, it is an abuse of the Almighty to believe in Him without using our resources properly, adequately and justly.

Experiencing both problems of excess (e.g., el-niño) and shortage of rain at different times, it is important to realize the need for harvesting rain for modernized irrigation farming.

Markets

This is another area that kills our agriculture. The government has left the issue of markets to the private sector which decides what to buy and at what price. Due to the poor infrastructure situation discussed above, transportation is a big challenge to most farmers; hence the few traders who are up to the challenge have to transport crops for them. This leads to a situation of monopoly, wherein those who took the challenge and risk are now free to set both the buying and the selling price once the produce is delivered to the market. Additionally, our farmers almost completely lack access to market information, and the monopoly is unbreakable. This puts our farmers at a terrible disadvantage, taking away any profitability they might have expected to get from the sweat of their labor.

Per capita income for the rural areas is estimated to be Tshs. 14,134 pa - a little less than the average per capita income of Tshs. 17,928 for mainland Tanzania and far lower than the average per capita of Tshs. 40,767 for Dar es Salaam. And according to Lazaro and Mdoe the only way to improve this situation is to improve the bargaining power of the producers, and I can relate to this as well.

In the few paragraphs above, one gets a picture of our agriculture which is the chief contributor to our economic development. Only 23% of land suitable for agriculture is used. 10% of this is cultivated by tractor. 35% of the cultivated land uses fertilizers. 57% of the crops get pest protection. 34% of this is non-chemical protection. Traders facing the challenge of the poor road situation come and purchase what has been salvaged in this very poor process, and impose their price.

Banking

Banking is another sector with a tremendous improvement over the past few years. On June 14th 1966, The Bank of Tanzania (BoT) was established after the National Assembly passed the Bank of Tanzania Act in December 1965. Tanganyika and Zanzibar had used the East African currency till then. The Bank was charged with carrying out all the traditional banking responsibilities of a central bank. Major changes were introduce in 1967, with the nationalization of all the commercial banks and placing them under the newly formed National Bank of Commerce (NBC), with the BoT as the supervisory authority, with the responsibility of issuing the national currency, which started circulating that same year.

Today, after decentralization and liberalization of the banking sector under commercial banks and foreign exchange Acts of 1992, Tanzania has an excellent network the banking sector from merchant banks, commercial banks, bureaux de change, a stock exchange and other related financial institutions. By the end of 2004 there were 22 registered commercial banks, some of which are international banks, with the biggest having 104 branches all over the country; 102 bureaux de change (22 of which are in Zanzibar); and 3 non-banking financial institutions (Bank of Tanzania). All these banks and bureaux de change are supervised by the Bank of Tanzania (source: BoT).

The improvement in the banking sector is not recorded only in the increase in the number of banks but also in the banking and financial services and operations. There has also been a lot of improvement in payment systems, financial markets, transfer of funds and international banking, business credits and loans, etc. As the banking sector speaks for itself, this is another area where development is clear and directly touching people in their day-to-day activities. A few more improvements are required, especially in strategy. We need to prioritize things for the benefit of the nation. One priority, as I have discussed in the agriculture section, is in connection to investment and extension of loans and credits to agricultural activities, especially in favor of small farmers.

In the history of banking, we also remember a few events where people lost or nearly did lose their money through bankruptcy of banks that caused anguish to some of us like the event of 1995 of the Meridian Bank. Greenland Bank followed suit; but BoT, as part of its core responsibilities, intervened and rescued customers' funds and supervised a refund during which time a similar event occurred in Uganda when the Greenland Bank went bankrupt. Bravo to our Central Bank.

Technology

Telecommunications

When former President Mkapa announced that Tanzania was entering the 21st century majestically he might have been thinking of telecommunications, for in no other area can this statement be closer to the truth. For a long time the telephone services in Tanzania presented the ordinary man and woman with nothing less than a nightmare. Some districts had only three to five phone lines, one for the district governor, one for the police, one for the security officer, one for the hospital, and maybe one for the local tycoon.

It was not uncommon to be kept on the line for hours waiting to be connected to the destination you were calling, or hear some voice interrupting you to ask you to hang up because someone else wanted to use the same line. Gone and forgotten are those surrealistic times in present day Tanzania. We had but Tanzania Postal and Telecommunication (TPTC) for all our postal and communication needs.

Today, the telecommunication industry has been revolutionized greatly and service providers are a matter of choice and taste. We have seen in the last ten years every kind of phone in Tanzania, and today, communication between different parts of the country, both urban and rural is not only plentiful but fast and comparatively cheap. In 1995 there were only two phone service providers and in 2004 this number grew to seven. One among these is TTCL that dominates the land line phone service; four other companies are cell phone service providers using underground technology while two others use satellite technology (source: URT). This is excellent progress as Tanzanians have among the fastest growth rates in the continent in this area. Almost two million Tanzanians own and use cell phones today.

Nonetheless, Tanzania has, to a large extent, remained a recipient of technology products rather than serving as a base of technological invention. A dilemma remains in most other areas of technology. Take geology, for instance, where we lack both expertise and machinery. Thus, although the mining sector has grown quite considerably in the past decade it is largely foreign companies that have dominated this sector. This has denied Tanzanians any measure of control over their resources and has caused widespread suspicion that foreigners are ripping Tanzanians off.

Williamson Diamonds mines in Mwadui Shinyanga, one of the oldest diamond mines in the world and the richest in East Africa, which has produced about 3,800 kg of diamonds for the past 65 years, is 75% owned by South African FIRM – De Beers - and only a quarter of the shares are owned by the Tanzanian Government (source: De Beers).

Production decreased appreciably for some time when the mine was fully owned by the government following the Arusha Declaration, because the government lacked the resources, both human and material to enhance productivity for the procurement of diamonds. The mine was very productive (about 10 times more) the first 25 years.

The mining sector should be a major area of activity bringing in huge benefits for our people if we only possessed the expertise requisite for its exploitation. But we have been unable to train professionals in the field, and the few professionals we have are not listened to. Furthermore there have been complaints that the agreements that have been entered into by government have not taken the interests of the country at heart but have rather tended to favor foreign investors, spelling a subsequent major loss for Tanzanians.

Tanzania is now said to be among the richest African countries in gold mining, after South Africa and Ghana. USD 592 million were obtained from gold in 2004. This was compared to about USD 2 million in 1995. More social services have been improved in places where there is gold.

But, notwithstanding these claimed benefits, it is still clear that Tanzania is only getting a pittance of what it really deserves. We also have to consider the very high price paid in these mines in terms of loss of lives and resources. The Bulyanhulu gold mine is a good example here, with all the accusations and denials concerning small-scale miners who were allegedly buried alive in an operation intended to clear the area for foreign investors. I, like many others failed to know if the Bulyanhulu saga was "fire or smoke". If it was fire, something is terribly wrong in our entire system; if it was just smoke, it was suspiciously so. It has not been possible to establish the authenticity of these claims. The open letter addressed to President Mkapa by the Lawyers' Environmental Action Team (LEAT) in 2001 articulated these claims very clearly. What this situation explains is that the mining sector has been more a source of controversy than prosperity for Tanzanians

But that is probably all we can get. We have few options for we are technologically-challenged. Our inability to handle these mines, man and exploit them has resulted in surrendering them to foreign forces which may have interests contrary to ours, and it has not helped any that our negotiators have tended to sign agreements that favor foreign interests.

Other areas of technology: computer technology; auto manufacturing technology; aircraft technology; bio-medical technology; bio-mechanical technology, forensic science; nanotechnologies and many other modern state-of-the-art technologies are completely beyond the grasp of Tanzanians and remain very much underdeveloped.

Developed nations depend heavily on technology. Those nations do not have supermen or extra-intelligent people; all they have is a deliberate interest and genuine effort in encouraging scientific and technological researches. These aspects have helped these nations understand that technology is a crucial aspect of development in this century. In fact economic development and technological advancement are so married together that separation of either from the other is inconceivable. We have to invest heavily in "quality education" and technology if we want development.

Infrastructure

Development Projects

Transportation infrastructure is among the five priority sectors under the Tanzania Poverty Reduction Strategy Paper (PRSP). This is an area that affects almost every other sector. For instance, we have seen what effects transport has in agriculture. A lot of emphasis has been placed on investment in many sectors, as seen above, but not enough effort has gone into the development of transportation infrastructure. That is why we must, from now on, concentrate our minds and efforts on this sector that is so crucial for all round development.

Our budget is still over 40% dependent on donors. The current budget allocation for development projects is below 20% and it has been so for the past couple of years, which means so little is done in economic and social development.

Under the first phase government, a good portion of the annual budget was reserved for development projects. Statistics indicate that with an exception of the 1964 - 1965 budget, most budget allocations had more than 30% allocated for development, with about 43.5% in 1975. It was during this period that major infrastructural projects were undertaken in different areas. Projects like Kilimanjaro, Mtwara and Mwanza Airports, the Tanzania-Zambia Railway Authority (TAZARA), Dar es Salaam port, many higher learning institutions (Sokoine Agriculture, Ardhi Institute, IDM Mzumbe, Ubungo Water Institute), and many industries, especially textile industries (Mwatex, Mutex, Kiltex, Sunguratex, and Urafiki) were accomplished in the first decade of the union. If the government had maintained the same trend in budgetary allocation to development projects a lot more development would have been achieved, but the contrary happened and our investment in development has taken a nosedive over the years.

Roads and Bridges

Our country has a total road network of more than 85,000 km., carrying about 75% of the country's freight and about 90% of passengers. Of the entire network, only 16% of the roads are considered to be in good condition and only 7% are paved. The situation is worse in rural areas where 60% of the roads are impassable due to lack of bridges or culverts and 90% are totally impassable during rainy seasons.

The poor conditions of the roads make for serious transportation problems. Though the Ministry of Works has been making visible efforts to improve the condition of the country's roads, it is clear that much, much more remains to be done on deficiency of our roads. Our attitude towards this problem is the archenemy. The evident abuse in such development projects like Integrated Road Project (IRP) sponsored by EC and the World Bank has cost us. Poor mobilization and misuse of road funds resulted in a slow-down of donor support back in 1999.

The semi-autonomous TANROADS, which was established as part of the vision 2025 in the second phase of IRP as an in-charge of implementation of road developments rehabilitation and maintenance using private contractors and consultants is currently trying to mend the wrongs. So far so good improvements - the challenge is now for the current administration to enhance TANROADS and make sure that it is not, as has been suggested in some quarters, infected with the dangerous socio-economic disease we have discussed.

The third phase government did an excellent job in the area of roads, especially in the southern zone that was lagging far behind in infrastructure. Many road projects have been completed and many more are underway, examples of which are the Mkapa Bridge, the 240 km road between Dar – Kimanzichana – Kibiti, and many others that connect Mtwara, Masasi, Tunduru, and Mbamba-bay (Songea) are relevant here.

Notwithstanding the improvement in our roads, as already noted, and in spite of all that seems to hold good promise for the future, we still have to worry about an important aspect of many of our roads, and that is the aspect of standards.

Under the second phase government passenger buses were restricted to day time travel after an increased number of road accidents, especially on the Dar-Mbeya and Dar-Arusha routes. Mr. Augustine Mrema, then Minister for Home Affairs pioneered this move and supervised it diligently. This was meant to decrease the number of road accidents due to recklessness. The recently reported accidents suggest that we did not solve this problem. Accidents happen at almost the same rate. By the present set of facts, it is estimated that for the past ten years more than five people died every single day because of road accidents. 42 others were injured everyday; some of them sustaining permanent disabilities. Just what is the problem?

The third phase government, under the Ministry of Communications and Transportation, introduced the unresearched speed governors. If anything this was a total disaster and chaos to Tanzanians from the word go. It was as if this exercise was for experimentation in Tanzania. But nobody seemed to have cared about the findings. It never was a viable scientific method of speed control. But for one reason or the other it was forced into a short existence. Bus owners were given an ultimatum. People, especially in Dar es Salaam marched on the streets because busses were sent to a few garages that were given "the tender" and at the end, it developed to be a huge corruption channel and left Tanzanians with more road accidents than speed governors!

According to the government's reports, accidents have been reduced by 6.6% in the past ten years, but this is hardly anything to write home about. We certainly can do better than that. There are just too many people dying unnecessarily on roads that are either too narrow or otherwise sub-standard, coupled with the recklessness of our drivers and the couldn't-care-less attitude of highway security authorities. The number of road users is increasing exponentially while our roads remain very narrow. The road signs are gone. Traffic lights have drowned in power rationing. We really need to revise these standards if we want to minimize death caused by road accidents. Technology can also be employed and play a major role in controlling and recording of road accidents. The use of things like EDRs – Event Data Recorders – may seem to us as luxury for now, but they have been proven to help in studying the causes of accidents, especially those caused by reckless drivers, and hence can lead to recommendations of what can be done.

Kigamboni

Another long-time dilemma for Tanzanians, especially the Dar es Salaam residents has been the issue of the Kigamboni crossing. For many years, more than 500,000 people living in Kigamboni have had trouble with their to-and-fro movements to the city center where most people work and attend school. The Kigamboni Ferry has been a problem both in terms of reliability of service and safety. Though records may not be readily available, there have been numerous accidents and deaths during perilous crossings from one shore to the other. There has been talk of installing a drawbridge over the creek, but one is unsure whether it is the finances or the politics that are delaying such a welcome move. Unfortunately this issue has also been politicized a lot and dirty deals have been made on the Kigamboni Ferry. Mv. Kigamboni and Mv. Alina have been stable now for the past decade or so; but there is still a problem of limitation of freedom because of the hours of operation with midnight imposing an effective curfew. Come then, and you will not cross. Now, that is not what Kigamboni residents want. We need a permanent solution. It has been suggested that the NSSF has plans not only to develop modern, luxurious real estate properties the other side of the creek, but also to make crossing a matter of choice: driving, cycling, or walking comfortably across the dream bridge.

The recent plans by government to purchase a larger boat with the capacity of 500 tonnes, which may carry up to 2000 passengers and more than 50 vehicles, are of course awaited curiously. This will enhance the current ferry capacity of less than 33% of the planned ferry.

Other crossings at Busisi in Mwanza, Kilombero in Morogoro, and the Ruvuma River have also caused many accidents, occasioning deaths; but plans of improvement and procurement of life-saving boats have regulated the situation somewhat. This is a job well done. We should keep it up though.

Corruption
Tanzania is being attacked by two very dangerous physical and socio-economic diseases. I have discussed the former at length. That is HIV/AIDS. I am going to discuss the latter in brief despite having made a mention somewhere as one of the failures of the third phase administration. That is corruption. Evidently, corruption persisted in all the three phases of government leadership, from Nyerere at independence, through Mwinyi, to Mkapa in the third phase administration and worse still in the current phase of administration. Magnitudes differed, as did the approaches taken to solve the problem, and yet the situation has been alarming in the last two phases of government.

According to An Overview of Benjamin Mkapa's First Five-Year by the Department of Politics and Public Administration of the University of Dar es Salaam, corruption is still one of the worst problems of our country. "Under the second president, Ali Hassan Mwinyi, corruption spiraled out of control and November 1994, donors froze aid to Tanzania fearing that the government had lost its ability to manage the state" (Kiley 1994). Under Mwinyi, Tanzania was consistently listed as one of the most corrupt nations in Transparency International's annual rankings. In the 1995 elections, the first multi-party elections in thirty years, corruption was the central issue, not only for the opposition, but for the ruling party CCM as well. At the beginning of Mkapa's rule it was predicted that matters were bound to improve, especially because of the campaign promises made by Mkapa himself and his foremost campaigner, Mwalimu Nyerere. Nonetheless, corruption has become one of the most glaring failures of the third phase government.

"Corruption is inimical to justice; I will not engage myself in corruption practices" This was one of the ten vows of TANU Creed, inherited by CCM, and which aimed at setting ethical standards for true leaders. And yet this is the one vow that most Tanzanian leaders have violated with impunity.

At one time the donor community was excited by rhetorical efforts made by the Mkapa administration on its intent to curb corruption, but this soon proved to be mere lip service, and at the end of the first five years, donors started to question the consensus between the declared intent to fight corruption and the effects of the anti-corruption efforts made by the administration -there was none. Despite prosecuting a couple of fall guys as a sop for many corruption activities by sending them to court, serious practical effort has been demonstrated even when rumors about corruption were in every local paper.

One mistake in the anti-corruption war was to underestimate the gravity and complexity of corruption. As I said earlier, the barking dog style was not sufficient to reduce corruption at its micro and macro levels. There are some Tanzanians who know not any other means of survival in Tanzania than the game of kitu kidogo (just a small thing). They believe Bongo is a land of playing smart. You do not stop these people by mere words of threats. In its numerous forms and complexity, corruption in Tanzania needed a long-term approach plan that would involve intensive and systematic research, study, and knowledge of exactly how to combat it at both levels (petty, grand). By the levels of corruption it means there is a level that involves even the "very elect" – the high officials in the government who would probably orchestrate the fight against it. Therefore it is a very tricky war. It is a war against the known and the unknown, the obvious and the concealed, the poor and the rich, the leaders and the followers, the educated and the unlearned, the law makers and the law breakers - all included. It is a complex and tricky thing because it is both a legal and moral issue. Therefore it required more than just the rhetoric approach that Mkapa's administration used.

What can we say then about corruption? Are we losers? Not necessarily; it is true we might have committed a colossal error; but I am made to believe that our error is not irretrievable. I suppose we still have the chance to minimize it if we mean to. We need a renewed zeal and commitment on this. The current administration needs to put together a plan to resolve this problem from the roots. Once again this would need intensive research and study of the problem so we could understand its breadth and depth. The next step is to know the causes, which unfortunately seem to range widely from low wages, unrealistically high fines, fees and taxes, bureaucracy, poor services in public institutions, poor working tools, dishonesty, and an urge for illegal riches.

Media

This is another area that has been more revolutionized than most sectors. It is clear that we have come a long way in the area of media. Up until 1994, when the Chairman and CEO of IPP Group, Reginald Mengi, was threatened death in a license war to show the world cup finals, Tanzania was probably the only country in the whole wide world without a television station, although the government of Zanzibar had already established a TV station as early as 1972. It wasn't until 1994 when we first watched local TV broadcasting. In the same year we had three private stations: Independent Television (ITV), Coastal Television Network (CTN), and Dar es Salaam Television (DTV). Private Radio stations were also a rare commodity, and all we had for our news and commentaries was the one and only government owned Radio Tanzania - Dar es Salaam (RTD). It was, no doubt, RTD became a very effective tool of political control and propaganda in the hands of TANU and later CCM, and their government. On the other hand though, RTD played an important role in building a strong, unified nation by promoting, among other things, the proper usage of Kiswahili.

The mushrooming of media instruments today offers an adequate testimony of the tremendous progress we have made in this area. We now take pride in the variety of flavors available in the media. We can choose and select which source to view, listen, or read. As of now, Tanzania has a total of well over one hundred daily and weekly papers. Not only that, but we also now have 32 radio stations (with Dar es salaam having the most, 15, Arusha 4, Mwanza and Morogoro 3 each, and others spread among other major towns), 63 television and cable stations plus 23 large internet service companies (source: URT) and of course untold number of small internet service providers.

This is good progress; but the issue here cannot be simply the number of newspapers and radio stations. Nor is it the televisions stations. Although numbers have their own importance, it is more about quality and credibility of information and the impartiality of writers/reporters. Someone once said, "The only role of the media is to tell the public which direction the cat has jumped. The public will take care of the cat." The media people should always keep this in mind as they write and report. We now are in the information age. Information is power. It is, therefore, important that those who are in the area of handling, processing, and disseminating information to realize the importance of their duty. Far from being an industry wherein those who could not make it elsewhere find their sustenance and survival, media is about providing that space of societal intercourse and dialogue, where ideas are synthesized and strategies weighed against each other with a view to harmonizing societal thinking and by so doing helping to chart out a future course of action for national development. Media can regulate and balance variations in society. A windshield is to a vehicle as the media is to a nation's economic development. If the windshield is so cracked and obscured, it makes the driving harder. Therefore we need a good clear windshield.

The media's role is one of unmatched importance in terms of regulating the connection between the government and the public and revealing the evils of either to the other. In one way it can help the government through its institutions to do its job by making known what would otherwise not be known. In the other way it helps the public to be aware of any abuse or misuse of public resources. Issues like Uhujumu uchumi, Kigamboni ferry scandal in the early 90s, OIC, the government extravagance in Rio De Janeiro conference, imported rice and wheat scandals, imported sugar scandal, tax exemption scandals, Zanzibar killings of 2001, NBC scandal and many other privatization-related scandals, gold mine scandals, illegal trade of logs of timber, government official's wife's false medical expenses abroad, many corruption scandals, container scandals, fire in government buildings, and many more untold stories can indicate how significant the role of media is in the development of a nation.

Mohammed Amin, a Kenyan photo-journalist died as one of the world's most famous journalists. His photo coverage on numerous issues made him an eminent journalist. He played a good role as a journalist and helped many families, especially in Ethiopia where famine had struck hard. No doubt this was his most important contribution as a journalist. The famine pictures in 1984 caught the world's attention with great sympathy. Ethiopia received its due attention after Amin had done his job well, although of course these pictures have been used negatively in some cases by the western media for their propaganda. Nonetheless, Amin, whose untimely death at the age of 53 in a hijacked plane crash in November 23rd, 1996, in Comoros Islands, which saddened most Africans, played an important role in journalism. Amin was nicknamed "the eye of Africa" by some writers. Now, the media in Tanzania should play as "the eye of Tanzania"

What is needed is fairness and reputation. Media practitioners need to foster integrity within their ranks. Some of them also need to move their focus away from trivial and sensational reporting to more challenging and socially constructive writing. Stories on the private lives and affairs of individuals may not in any way contribute to the development of our society, economically or socially. It seems we have read more than enough about which Kigogo (bigwig) has been getting it on with which woman. It is time now to read and hear worthwhile information.

Freedom of Press/Speech

Freedom of Press in Tanzania is another topic that would merit another entire book of the same volume as this one, so I am not going to get into great details of that too; but I just want to say very briefly but emphatically that we have a long way to go before we can claim to have achieved acceptable levels in the area of speech and press freedom. Fortunately we have no alternative in this case, because freedom of speech is among those absolutely crucial non-negotiable attributes of a democratic society that is to develop and especially in multiparty politics.

But up to this point, we have witnessed so many things that hinder the endeavors to build a free nation in speech and press. Detained editors/reporters; banned publications; verbal, sexual, and sometime physical abuse of writers and reporters; not to mention the withholding of cooperation on the part of officials who keep crucial information under wraps. These are some of the troubles the media people endure from day to day.

This has also turned out to be one of many avenues for corruption and bribes. In some cases newsmen and women have been known to succumb to the lure of bribery because they need to make ends meet in a situation where they are poorly paid because they work for hardly solvent media houses. Circulation figures are still very low even for the most read papers, and advertising is still undeveloped in the country. Major stories of great public interest have been killed because they involved some "big shot" who could pay his way out by bribing the broke reporter on the beat as well as his equally broke editor. This constitutes a major hindrance to the freedom of the Press and freedom of expression as it hobbles the best efforts of those who want us to have an effective media as the most solid guarantor of free speech and expression.

On the other hand it has been noticed that those in positions of authority have a hard time taking criticism or the simple stating of facts they may not want known by the general public. They have to learn to accept facts and criticism, for we are in an era where it will no longer be possible to suppress these for long.

This said, it is still important to emphasize that press freedom can be a double-edged sword. The media also has an important role to play in another sense. As former president Mkapa has said many times, we need serious people in this area. And as one of the prominent journalists, Jenerali Ulimwengu, remarked at a meeting with journalists in Bagamoyo on May 2004, the press plays a very important role in the development of a country and in promoting harmony and peace, but "the worst threat to press freedom comes from the journalists themselves."

The press should not be abused and misused to mislead the general public in the interests of the few. The overall goal of the media should not only be geared to money making. Ethics should be safeguarded. Apart from the importance of upholding ethical behavior, it should be clear that there are so many Tanzanians who either cannot afford, or are not interested in following current affairs through foreign media, and that these rely almost exclusively on domestic media. To do them justice our media must strive to present its news, views and commentaries in an honest, unbiased and helpful way, without willfully abusing their trust. Deliberate efforts need to be made here to control the random handling, or rather mishandling, of information and news; such efforts include more rigorous training, strict gate-keeping systems and the inculcation of codes of ethics generated by media practitioners and media owners themselves.

5

Culture and Religion

Tanzanian Culture

I once read in one of the numerous discussion forums present in the internet today that Tanzania has no culture as a nation! Initially the claim sounded so shallow to me, but the writer was good in intensifying his argument by providing facts that almost caught me.

He continued by saying that there are many indigenous groups that have many different traditions in Tanzania but there is nothing standard as a Tanzanian culture. Despite sharing many common habits as Tanzanians with which we may identify ourselves sometimes and some of which are articulated in the Arusha Declaration, which of course very few of us may have the boldness to advocate its validity in this anti-Nyerereism era, we are still a very diverse society, the claim continued.

I quickly realized that the writer missed a key point. That in spite of the traditional and customary diversity of Tanzanians, Tanzania has a culture. The only problem our culture has is the dilution made by copying foreign habits.

The definition of culture used here is taken from Random House Webster's Dictionary that means the "ways of living built up by human groups and transmitted to succeeding generations." If Tanzanians have maintained peace and stability socially and politically as a nation through the years there must have been some way these people have lived harmoniously and passed these ways down the generations. So claiming that we have no culture is absolutely wrong.

Tanzanians have been identified as unified peoples in their diversity whose linguistic weapon, Kiswahili, which is also part of our culture, has had the effect of overshadowing all divisions and differentiations arising out of the ethnic categorizations. Tanzanians have been identified as peacemakers. Many tribes in the country cannot divide Tanzanians. Tanzanians have been identified as generally kind and polite people. Many social teachings with emphasis on cultural issues have been administered through traditional musical dances, songs, proverbs and storytelling - many of these emphasizing morals, unity, bravery, generosity, peace and familyhood, which characterize a Tanzanian people. These teachings are then put into practice in life's important activities and events like marriages, deaths, etc. These events have been celebrated in unique fashions that emphasize unity. Tanzania is unified in her diversity through a strong culture of familyhood and kindness. Although different ethnic groups may have different ways of expressing their feelings regarding all aspects of life, still they all subscribe to a certain general etiquette of peace, love and care for the next person.

In spite of connection to other external communities, Tanzania managed to embrace her culture down the ages. Most visitors and tourists have been impressed by what we offer them through the musical dances as the first gift.

Nevertheless, important cultural intrusions have meant that some aspects of foreign cultures have imposed themselves on our culture in such a way that they have distorted it and made it seem as if Tanzania indeed has no culture of her own.

Copying and Imitation

The economic problems experienced by our country over the past three decades triggered an unprecedented exodus of Tanzanians overseas. Many people who left to go and seek greener pastures with a distinct cultural identity came back with ambiguous foreign cultures. Some have been transformed into different individuals and others completely wrecked-out and written-off culturally and morally. Our dependency in foreign aids to supplement our economy has also many times forced us into accepting things that we would otherwise never choose. Therefore as a result of this go-take-everything-and-bring-it-back-home practice, Tanzania has found itself in a matrix of integration of a very complex, and yet superficial culture.

In the same context of corrupted cultural lifestyle, Tanzanians have also developed many heterogeneous habits that are not typical to our surroundings and historical identity. Earlier in the book I have discussed the problem of imitation. Copying and imitating foreign traditions and cultures has dominated the minds of many Tanzanians over the years, especially the younger generation. It has almost become some kind of a cultural infection. No wonder, we hear claims of our country having no culture of her own. We imitate everything from everywhere: dressing, music, behavior, and lifestyle generally.

Morals and Values

The result of this complex integration of foreign cultures has been an acute loss of morals and values in our society. Morals here being defined as "the human conduct so far as it is freely subordinated to the ideal of what is right and wrong" from the Catholic Encyclopedia.

In our very same society where there used to be a huge gap and a crystal clear difference between right and wrong, good and evil, a very thin line exists in between the two extremes today. This makes it difficult for our young men and women to navigate through the complexities of today's society. We live in the era of relativism. Right or wrong, good or evil have become very relative terms – their definitions differing from person to person. Habits and practices like homosexuality, prostitution, teen-sex, public disrespect for elders, rape, violence, pornography, drug-abuse, profanity and many other social crimes were never acceptable in our societies; and would receive reprimand from every side of our society; but today we seem to be more comfortable with these practices. There are even advocates who would like to see such shameful behaviors tolerated and accepted.

The consequence of entertaining these immoral practices is a high price we pay. Most of these result in direct or indirect destruction of members of our society. We have seen from elsewhere the growing number of problems as a result of loss of morals and values. A people that has no morals, has lost the most important aspect of humanity. We need to build a society that does not glorify violence and immorality, which is one of the very rewarding roles we, as a nation, can accept. We have the advantage to witness the destruction that has been brought by immorality in other societies. These societies, having failed to maintain values and morals, resorted into more and more legal laws in the fight against social ills, but the more the draconian laws they put in place the worse the social problems became.

The legalistic path has not solved their problems, but has complicated them. There are so many laws that the laws contradict themselves. It is crucial to understand that there is no amount of laws (as long as the laws cannot penetrate the human mind) that can stop an evil person from thinking and acting evil. John Adams, former President of the USA once said "no government armed with power capable of contending with human passions unbridled by morality and religion". This means there has never been a government powerful enough, on its own, to compete with human passions. It is therefore more important to have a well brought-up society that understands the difference between right and wrong and good and bad than have a vast number of laws in a society that has completely lost a sense of right or wrong.

In order to help our nation and protect our people we need to emphasize the importance of values and the things we believe in through academic curriculums and social teachings. Without the temptation to subordinate the importance of legal laws, and without causing any misunderstanding that this opinion seeks even remotely to despise the legal system, we need not overestimate it either; after-all "the law ignores the deepest needs of humanity and compromises the liberty of the people". As Tanzanians we need to develop our moral code and stand for it. We need to develop our own moral code and respect our beliefs. We have to refuse being recipients of values and beliefs from other people who nonetheless have failed morally.

The problem is catalyzed by the demands of life that has necessitated the abrupt change in rhythm of lifestyles of many people. Life at a family level has made an about turn, the result of which is that the importance of parenting has been subordinated and has been replaced by office jobs and other less important social activities.

The video games madness that in most cases advocates violence and crimes has intruded our homes and has turned out to be the most common baby-sitting tool. The result of this is zero parental guidance; and therefore the imported video games are causing pollution to our kids' minds by planting evil thoughts and destructive ideas in their psyches.

We are living in a culture that is too deeply drowned in home entertainment. More than any generation of the past, home entertainment affects our life so extensively today. Home entertainment in the form of television and video has grown significantly and can no longer be taken as lightly as a mere past-time but a serious domestic issue that requires very careful and very close follow up and guidance to our children taking into consideration the influence the visual media can impose on a human mind, especially the delicate but curious minds of our children.

Very high technology is now used to bom the human mind with satellite video entertainment at homes, in cars, and even in offices and all public places. Entertainment is just part of life, but in our society today life has become but part of entertainment. Unfortunately we all know, as Stephen Covey puts it, "Like body, television is a good servant but a poor master."

Unfortunately parenting today has turned out to mean less the provision of moral, spiritual and intellectual upbringing than the provision of totally unnecessary and nefarious toys, including toy-guns to the youngest members of our society. Most parents have chosen to distance themselves from training kids, the result of which is most of the kids have been left to house maids and in-house games. And they are overburdened with mind-numbing entertainment and all sorts of commercialized children's games. Children are left with no quality time for emotional and moral development and hence suffer a complete loss of direction. I am not quite sure where and when the next turning point is going to be; but again, like I said there is a need to bring up a society that doesn't take pride in glorification of immorality.

In 2003 there arose a controversy between the government and the people because of a group of 100 homosexuals who wanted to tour Tanzania. This was immoral, unethical, illegal, and unacceptable in the Tanzanian community, especially when it was to be made public. All the government wanted was money; and it did not make any difference whether the 100 dollars was from a homosexual or from a heterosexual. This was a clash in both the culture and law. Homosexuality is both legally and morally a problem in Tanzania. Bad enough it was the government that was giving the 100 homosexuals the go ahead. To the government it was: if it is good for our GDP, it is good for Tanzanians. That line of thinking in this particular case and other morally-sensitive issues is wrong. Good enough the homosexuals realized the resentment and the tension that existed among the Tanzanian community; so they never set foot on the land at least that is what is believed. In spite of this, however, it is sad to say that homosexuality is gaining ground in Tanzania nowadays.

I was reading disturbing statistics that indicate a growing number of Tanzanians being arrested abroad in connection to immoral issues; and I thought to myself, well, this is a nation that had built such a high international reputation that other nationalities used to disguise themselves as Tanzanian citizens in order to enter easily into other countries. Today, the opposite is true. It was recorded for instance that, between 1989 and 1991, about 470 Tanzanians were arrested abroad in connection to illegal drug trafficking. In Tanzania itself, the problem has become so acute that tons and tons of marijuana and activan, mandrax, nizoral, heroine, and cocaine are being seized by police every now and then; but many others go unnoticed. From 1990 to 1995 there were 12,465 court cases of drug abuse and trafficking. Until recently such cases had been very rare indeed.

It is good to learn that a commission was established in 1997 to particularly deal with the problem of drug trafficking in Tanzania. But this is one of those areas that a commission or any government agency cannot, on its own, manage to combat every crime without full support of its citizens. Citizens should be part of the war against drug abuse. Drug abuse is extremely dangerous to both the user and the rest of society. Its health and mental effects are terrible.

Language
As I mentioned in the introductory part of this book, our country has more than a hundred local languages corresponding to ethnic groups. This is not necessarily a plus in cohesion or political stability, as has

been observed in numerous African countries. But Tanzania has been exceptional in having Kiswahili as a lingua franca for all these groups.

Kiswahili developed as a unique and dynamic mélange of the Bantu languages of the interior with the numerous languages brought to the East African coast by various trade winds. Of special note among these languages is Arabic, although other languages also found their way into the Kiswahili melting pot, e.g., Hindu, Urdu, Gujarat, Farsi and Portuguese.

Although most communities in East Africa, from the coast to the hinterland, all the way to eastern Congo, used Kiswahili in various shapes and guises, it was in Tanganyika, later Tanzania, that serious efforts were made to standardize, rationalize and universalize Kiswahili, first by the colonial authorities and later by the independence government. It became the national and official language soon after independence and has grown tremendously ever since, buoyed mainly by a homogeneous political discourse dominated by TANU and, later, CCM. Swahili is now said to be spoken by well over 100 million people in the world but Tanzanians speak it the best. It is the most widely spoken African language.

Because of its widespread and growing use, Swahili is used in many international broadcasting stations like Radio South Africa, BBC (England), Voice of America (USA), Radio Deutschewelle (Germany), Radio France Internationale (RFI), Radio Moscow International (Russia), Radio Cairo (Egypt), China Radio International (CRI) and many other stations in Japan, India, and Sudan; and it is now the official language of the African Union. Swahili is now in the curriculum of most Universities in the world.

This was possible because all the phases of Tanzanian government put emphasis on this language, including the colonial administration, which prioritized the use of Kiswahili for effective communication, in the case of the colonialists for effective control and, in the case of the post-independence government for rapid development.

The first president, Julius Nyerere was an ardent scholar of Kiswahili, who even translated two of William Shakespeare's plays into Kiswahili. The second president, Ali Hassan Mwinyi, was an erstwhile Kiswahili teacher in his younger day and he took delight in counseling his audiences on the proper use of Kiswahili words and phrases. Mr. Mkapa is a linguist by profession and his articulate ability in the use of Kiswahili was also a good factor. He is believed to have popularized some Kiswahili words. These people helped to enhance the status of the language and to make it recognized internationally as a linguistic force to be reckoned with, while at home the language further cemented the foundations of nationhood. We have a huge interest in maintaining and developing this language as the foremost unifying factor, not only for Tanzania, but also for our neighbors as we work together for greater integration.

Traditions

There are many Tanzanians today that are ashamed of their traditions, some of whom deny their origins because they feel embarrassed by some of their old traditions that they find outmoded. Yet some of these traditions represent stages of social and cultural development our people had to go through, and there should be nothing embarrassing about them. To be ashamed of our culture and traditions is to refuse our heritage and so our identity. While it is an inescapable fact that change is important in every area of human life, it is also important to respect our roots. It is essential to understand that there is nowhere a superior culture.

The importance of the traditions is obviously lost on the younger generations, but those who had the opportunity to live in our traditional societies when they still practiced their old ways of life had the chance to learn about the usefulness of these traditions and the role they played in keeping the society together and inculcating their moral values in younger generations.

These traditions made it easy for interpretation and implementation of values. People believed and practiced the same values. There were consistent sets of guidelines. This made learning easy for the children because every society member believed the same set of values; and every moral teaching pointed to the same direction. There were fewer but good choices. In the contrary, we are now living in the world flooded with choices. Choices are good only when necessary; but making up ten choices among which nine are harmful choices is not wholesome morally. Some things were never meant to change; or else it is the result of an obvious moral dilemma.

While there are many traditions from many ethnic groups, let me refer briefly to one tradition from the Kurya tribe of Mara region, and this is a custom that has excited a lot of discussion among sociologists and many observers. This is the institution of dowry. The practice of paying a bride price to the bride's (in some cases to the groom's) parents is an old and time honored practice, not only in Tanzania but all over the world, and it is meant to signify goodwill and appreciation to the parents. Moreover, dowry was also used to signify that the person proposing was responsible, independent and probably industrious enough to be entrusted with a spouse, or at least from a family with such characteristics. Cows were used to symbolize these aspects.

This has been one of the oldest Kurya traditions. Dowry was not supposed to take any rigid form or to be of a certain value. The number of cows to be offered was totally dependent upon agreement of the two sides. The validity of this tradition has diminished as years have gone by, because of inter-marriages and socio-economic development. Many other traditions were practiced in different societies in Tanzania. Polygamy has been another famous tradition that still exists to date. Another tradition has been that of circumcision of both boys and girls and many others that are obviously overtaken by time, knowledge and understanding but this is where we came from.

These traditions have, however, been mistakenly interpreted and misrepresented. It has been argued in some quarters that these practices have been a major cause of domestic problems, especially the violation of equality of rights. Dowry, for instance, is claimed to be a major source of abuse among married couples. While these claims may have a minimal amount of truth relating to some individual cases, domestic abuse and violation of equality are common problems, with or without bride price. In some cases women are said to be victims of abuse even in societies where it is the women who pay the dowry.

Religion

Tanzania has two major religions: Christianity and Islam. Many other religions also exist. None of these religions is national.

The late Nyerere said he had a difficult time at the beginning trying to advocate the philosophy of Tanzania having no religion, especially to the religious leaders. This was because of the misunderstanding that would be caused with this deep and powerful philosophy. Some religious leaders thought that Nyerere was about to start advocating atheism. However, what Nyerere meant was that Tanzania has no state religion, meaning that Tanzania was not going to be governed by a specific religious belief. He wanted people to have freedom of worship without state interference while electing leaders without bias in belief or affiliation – true separation of state and religion.

As part of building the society Nyerere also played a very good role in creating tolerance among different beliefs. Tanzanians mix in religion just as they mix in tribes without chaos. People inter-marry across religious lines just like they do across tribal lines. People have also enjoyed unlimited freedom of worship all along. It is imperative to cite the success in freedom of worship and individual choice of belief as one of the major successes of our country's administration.

6

Political Situation

Peace and Stability

As I, and most other writers and speakers have said numerous times, Tanzania is peaceful and stable socially and politically. However, that does not mean complete absence of chaos or instability. Neither should it mean Tanzanians should rest on this success and do nothing in this area. All it means is that some people worked hard in days gone-by to create the situation of peace and stability that is enjoyed today. We are the beneficiaries of the blood, sweat and tears of those who made sure that we live in stability. More effort should be made not only to maintain, but also enhance the inherited peace.

I remember one of many speeches of the late Mwalimu Nyerere in which he cautioned about laxity concerning the issue of peace. He urged hard work instead of wallowing in the luxury created by the peaceful environment. There is obviously a problem here: stepping with our own feet with full weight of pride right on top of the very peace we are supposed to nurture. It is no doubt we will spoil it.

While it may not be proper to point fingers to the political changes that we have undergone in the last decade, it is reasonably fair to conclude that some people in both the ruling and the opposition parties seem to not be ready for peaceful political challenges. First, there has been a problem of truly accepting the changes. Many, especially those in authority, still uphold the one-party tradition and find it hard to let go of it, just as it was easy to get the Israelites out of Egypt but extremely difficult to get Egypt out of the Israelites, it was easy to get into multipartyism but it has been very tough to let go the unipartyism; and so we fail to embrace the changes wholeheartedly. This has led to some leaders within the ruling party develop a deep-seated suspicion against people in the opposition as though the latter were somehow disloyal to the nation.

Although CCM as the ruling and only party at the time of the re-introduction of multi-party politics in 1992 was instrumental in effecting that process it is hard to believe that CCM itself was ready for those changes.

Notwithstanding public declarations to the effect that the opposition is accepted and welcome, actions by those in power tend to demonstrate the contrary, and since actions speak louder than words, it is concluded that perhaps most of our leaders were really forced into accepting these changes. This was most emphatically demonstrated during the first two multiparty elections, during which we witnessed dramatic levels of political immaturity, such as the use of gruesome footage of massacres in neighboring countries in an apparent effort to suggest to the electorate that voting for the opposition would lead to bloodshed. That was very improper and misleading.

Another problem in this area is our tendency to over-celebrate "the peace and tranquility" that we currently enjoy, singing about this situation so much that we have become propagandists on the matter rather than realists who can do a hardnosed analysis of the peace we so boast about. It is true that we currently enjoy peace, but we should understand that peace comes at a cost. Rather than continue to sing about the existing peace we should be busy looking into ways to maintain it and make it sustainable. Peace can only exist if there is justice. But as evidenced in some real-life incidents in Tanzania, justice is the biggest challenge. Right here a big question comes to mind: is it possible to be a peaceful society without justice? Definitely, no. So what we, Tanzanians, refer to very frequently and proudly as peace may just mean the absence of war, which is not necessarily peace, for peace is not a relationship of nations. It is a condition of mind.

In this nation there is still a big difference between an offense committed by one citizen and the same offense committed by another citizen of a supposedly different social class. There is also a big difference between the treatment of a "rich criminal" and the treatment of a "poor criminal". There can be no claim of peace when there is no justice, and it is important to ensure that the members of the lowest class in the country enjoy the same justice as those in the elite brackets. In Tanzania, we have not come to that point yet.

Selflessness is an uncommon noun that I want to use to discuss a very common problem - selfishness - the root of all evil.

At the beginning of his presidency, Mr. Mkapa promised, among many other things, to deal firmly with anyone, especially those among the leadership domain, who had amassed illicit wealth, and called on all the leaders to follow his example and publicly declare their wealth and how they came into it. It is hard to say how this idea died, and who buried it. But it is still a mystery to many.

This was perhaps the most unpopular idea of the third phase government. It basically lacked support with the ruling clique around Mkapa. Any of the following reasons could have been responsible for this lack of support: one, either most of those in power who were supposed to implement the idea would be the "victims" of any serious attempt to implement it, so they were reluctant and played dumb. Or two, it was probably inconvenient and irksome in the sense that we would have had to go back into the history lines of so many individuals within the regime, which would also be suggesting that at some time, somehow our government had gone on vacation. Or three, probably it was considered an affront to personal freedom. In any case, this exercise would have been very costly to the nation, as it would have meant going back to the history line and probe so many people's archives, with the possibility of aggravating corruption without necessarily producing any worthwhile outcomes.

Even though we did not go back into history and dig up ancient skeletons, we could at least have resolved to start afresh, at that moment, and commit ourselves anew to the fight against corruption. But people who had anticipated a new beginning with the Mkapa regime were soon disillusioned as they realized that the rhetoric was not to be matched by action. Perhaps Mr. Mkapa was compromised, who knows? Yet illicit wealth is among many old socio-economic problems of our country that require a permanent solution. Going back twenty, thirty years questioning the legality of one's possessions, might seem both cumbersome and unpopular, but wouldn't looking ahead and trying to do a serious job of curbing this surely be beneficial to our society and our fledgling economy?

All the same it is surprising that little attention was paid to this problem in the dying years of the Mkapa era, although it was Mkapa's main campaign plank in 1995. Unexplained personal wealth was one of the major concerns of the Mkapa regime when it took over, but it was soon realized that the regime's bark was far worse than its bite.

Thirdly, we also have shown very little capacity in laying any foundation for the continuation of our good fortunes. Again, let us refresh our memories, even though they may remind us of bitter experiences: one event was that of 2001 in Zanzibar when opposition political party members protested the general election alleging that it was not a free and fair election. Furthermore it was believed that their candidate had more votes the ruling party's candidate was however announced the winner. This represents a big and indelible scar on the history of our nation, and which serves to remind us of how little we are prepared to deal with political problems, which might eventually wipe out the peace and tranquility we speak of so much.

According to the 180-page report by Brigadier General (rtd) Hashim Mbita's commission, the Zanzibar killings were done by "ill-intentioned and under-trained police". Yes, ill-intentioned and under-trained! Otherwise we would not have heard of rape cases in the same scenes. Neither should we have seen the level of brutality that Jenerali Ulimwengu showed us on television and costed him his citizenship. He was ours until he stood boldly for this inconveniencing truth.

Being peaceful includes being compassionate and tolerant to one another. Peace does not start and end in having no problems; but extends to seeking harmonious solutions to presumably most complicated or most absurd demands. It should prevail in times of trouble too. If we only have peace in the absence of problems, that does not qualify us to be a "Haven of Peace". Everybody can use guns to kill, but the same should not pretend to be peaceful after usage of guns to stop demonstrators who were defenseless. That is to say that the beatings, the killings, and the abuses were an unnecessary extreme step.

On the other hand, though, with reference to Brigadier Mbita's report, we need to be very careful to distinguish who is well trained, who is under-trained and who is completely untrained, between the ones giving orders and those receiving orders and act. I remember an incident in Dodoma in 2003, where some people suffocated in a cell-room. Junior police officers were held responsible for the issue; but what would those poor officers do if their seniors did not provide them with enough facilities to accomplish their assigned tasks? The Zanzibari issue looks the same to me. Whoever did the beatings and the killings was just blindly carrying out the orders. Proof was in the zeal with which the senior officials under the President himself protected the brutal acts. As if that was not enough many commanders were promoted immediately after the incident.

This shows that there is a serious problem in our police force administration. If the police force has to assure peoples' safety and security, it should have nothing less than well trained officers.

Despite the fact that our leaders feel very confident that they did a good job to stop the riots/demonstrations by all the powers they had, it should be understood that it was not the best and the only way. The Zanzibari problem was probably complicated to our leaders, but it was not all that complex. I look at it as a minor political problem any nation with politically mature leaders should expect. So, if solving minor problems involves taking of peoples' lives in tens (tens because I really never knew what was the exact number of people killed due to multiple contradicting reports), and injuring hundreds of others, how then shall we react when major problems come our way? Our leaders kept saying that the number was smaller than publicized as though this makes it sound any nicer. It doesn't - just as it does not make it any more acceptable because even if it was one person killed, that would still be one life too many lost for a very unjust cause.

The rightful and legitimate use of force may be acceptable; but it must be exercised with caution and within legal and just parameters – when and only when it is absolutely necessary; but irresponsible killing of people, especially fellow citizens, cannot be a choice, among the methods of stopping a problem of that scope in a country like Tanzania whose signature is peace, and that has gained for itself international reputation and respect as a peacemaker. Dr. Martin Luther, King Jr., an American revolutionary once wrote: "Man was born into barbarism when killing his fellow man was a normal condition of existence. He became endowed with conscience. And he has now reached the day when violence toward another human being must become as abhorrent as eating another's flesh." From: Why We Can't Wait, 152. This is an era of human life when human beings are considered to be too intelligent to practice barbarism.

It is the feeling of most people, that there were still other options at the government's disposal that would solve the problem harmoniously.

Again here, it is completely wrong to just look at one side of the coin. The opposition side has almost an equal share of importance in contributing to the peace and development of the nation as does the ruling side. Their conduct is of high interest to the general public as those in power. In this case opposition parties should be well prepared with sound opposition and hence positive contribution to the nation. Every step they make should be of help to all the people; and not to a few leaders who have had the merits to start a political party. It has been more than a decade now since the re-introduction of multi-partyism in the country, but I am not very sure if enough effort has been made to make the opposition side strong enough for a meaningful challenge. I am afraid also that in that time we have experienced more political problems than were necessary. I hate chaos. I feel that opposition needs to revisit the very reasons for its existence and conform to them. Our nation has been a one party state since the 1960s; so we need keen people to take us smoothly through this process. Otherwise opposition will be more trouble to Tanzanians than it is help. Chaos is the last thing anyone would ever wish for Tanzanians.

Over the years and through the ages, we have been very good hosts of people who have completely lost hope of any meaningful life because of chaos from countries torn apart by social and political conflicts. In recent years, our country has been a refuge for people from South

Africa, Namibia, Uganda, and many others from Congo, Rwanda and Burundi in recent years. With the help of the United Nations High Commissioner for Refugees (UNHCR), Tanzania has hosted millions of refugees. With that amount of experience we know exactly the pains riots can inflict on peoples' lives. We know exactly the damage that may be caused by riots because we have experienced it, though second-handedly. We have witnessed the numbers of people who lost their lives in Rwanda, Burundi, Somalia, Congo, Uganda, Namibia, Liberia, Sudan and elsewhere because of riots, and know exactly the misery that can be caused by political and social differences. These people did not just choose to start killing each other. A little difference of opinion between two individuals/sides may result in such massive destruction of innocent people in presumably peaceful societies if intolerance cannot be controlled. Let us watch carefully. Political opposition is never social hatred. We need to respect the differences of our opinions.

Most opposition leaders have set their minds on the presidency. We cannot all be presidents; but we all need to serve our nation. Becoming the president of the country is not the only way one can serve this nation. Rather offering constructive criticism may help ease the burden of leadership. Opposition should strive to be credible and strong enough to make good challenges. Opposition is politically meant to bring balance to policy-making and undertakings. We expect the opposition leaders to understand also that the political parties are not for individual gains (fame and popularity); nor are they for disturbing peace in the country but instead are for posing needful challenges and helping the ruling government to see what it would otherwise not see. All allegations and accusations should be handled very peacefully and in a politically mature manner. And criticism should only be for the benefit of the general public and not for that of a few individuals.

Opposition should not be confused with revenge of some old deeds or personal hatred. Leaders of political parties should take time to employ more innovative and creative methods of challenging the ruling party rather than causing unreasonable and ineffective confrontations that cost peoples' lives in the end.

International Relations
Since the first phase government our international relations have been very credible. Our involvement in the liberation of other African countries has been commendable. Our involvement in seeking peace and stability in other countries has helped many people. Our willingness to accept and accommodate refugees by hundreds of thousands, despite many problems we have endured, has given many people a second

chance in life. The stories of Rwanda and Burundi are obvious cases to every African, of how Tanzania played an important role to make the world a better place for some people and making sure that peace is maintained. According to the 2004 report of the Foreign Ministry, our international relations are better now than any other time in history. The report by the Ministry says that we "had neither open nor any concealed enemy" by the end of ten years of the third phase government. Our diplomatic missions abroad are doing a good job, especially in the third phase government where the mission of our diplomacy changed into commercial diplomacy to attract international investors to the country. This is one of the few areas where statistics have coincided with the reality. Mkapa had worked as a diplomat for many years. Mr. Kikwete, following Mkapa as President, was in foreign affairs 10 years continuously prior to his presidency. They both had good knowledge of what exactly had to be done in our diplomatic relations.

Tanzania had only a few embassies in 1964. By the year 2004 Tanzania has had thirty full embassy offices in thirty countries. The embassies in United Emirates, Dubai, Rwanda, and Burundi were established between 1999 and 2002.

General Elections

I have written in earlier paragraphs that free and fair election is one of the most significant goals we need to achieve. There is a serious problem that causes the cry from most politicians, especially those on the opposition side. Although many a times these complaints are left out as trash, it is reasonable to say that we need to improve this situation for the reasons given below. Tanzanians need to maintain the peaceful political atmosphere we have enjoyed for a long time. We need to play fair games in politics. While enjoying our similarities, we should respect and accept our diversities in ideas, beliefs, and ideologies. Opposition was welcomed in Tanzania in quite a unique fashion. It should be maintained in the same unique fashion. We need not see people demonstrating on streets every now-and-then for things we can handle peacefully and diplomatically. I feel such pity and an so disturbed when seeing my fellow Tanzanians being beaten, sometimes killed like wild animals for just being different. That is a cost no person can afford to pay. We need to respect our differences and our rights as human beings and most importantly the right to live.

Let me put down some proposals that the authorities may wish to work with and correct wherever we did wrong.

National Electoral Commission (NEC) and Zanzibar Electoral Commission (ZEC)

There have been a number of complaints about the National Electoral Commission (**NEC**). There are complaints not only regarding its formation and structure but indeed its performance and credibility. While some of these claims are unjustifiable, it is evidently clear that efforts need to be made to improve, especially the performance of this Commission. It is important that the Commission's ultimate goal be to increase public confidence in the democratic process of election; and excellence in electoral matters is the only sure way to gain public confidence. However its structural establishment is still questionable to most democracy-loving individuals and patriots. I personally feel that the concern here is genuine and legitimate.

Article 74 of the 1977 Constitution of the United Republic of Tanzania provides for the establishment of the National Electoral Commission. Elections Act 1 of 1985 as amended in 1990 and 1992 of this article gives the president the powers to appoint all the seven (7) members of the NEC without prior advice or proposal from anybody else. It is the President, period.

On the other side of the union, there is also the Zanzibar Electoral Commission (**ZEC**) whose commissioners are appointed in a similar manner. Here lies the real problem. Most people are skeptical about having the Commission appointed and being responsible to the President. They fear that this could create loop-holes of irregularities and malpractices in a country very young in democracy such as Tanzania. The situation may be worse when a President is running for the second term. Most countries' constitutions have made provisions for appointment of electoral commissioners by committees, parliaments, or the judiciary and the same are given enough independent powers to minimize the possibility of malpractices. Even in cases where a President has to appoint the commissioners, it is after an advice/proposal or later confirmation by other bodies/committees, or with some limitations. A good example is the US where the President appoints the members of the Federal Electoral Commission (**FEC**), but he/she does not have the authority to appoint more than three (among the six) commissioners from one political party. Yet these appointments have to be confirmed by the Senate.

In the Republic of Korea the "**National Election Commission (EC)** is independent constitutional agency commensurate in status with the National Assembly, the Executive Branch of the government, Courts of Justice, and the Constitutional Court." This is to say that the

Electoral Commission in Korea is at the same level as both the executive and the legislative branches and as such it is not under any of the government branches.

In **Botswana** the "Independent Electoral Commission (IEC) is comprised of seven (7) members headed by a Chairperson and Deputy Chairperson, who are a judge of the High Court and a legal practitioner respectively. The two are appointed directly by the Judicial Service Commission. The Judicial Service Commission also appoints five (5) other members from a list of persons recommended by the All-Party Conference."

In **Canada**, "Elections Canada is an independent, non-partisan agency reporting directly to Canada's Parliament. The position of Chief Electoral Officer (CEO)," who is the chief commissioner, "is appointed by a resolution of the House of Commons. He or she reports directly to Parliament and is thus completely independent of the government of the day and all political parties."

In **Papua New Guinea, the "Electoral Commissioner** is appointed by the Governor-General as Head of State on the advice of the Electoral Commission Appointments Committee which is made up of the Prime Minister, or a Minister nominated by him, who shall be Chairman, the Leader of the Opposition or, in his or her absence the Deputy Leader of the Opposition the Chairman of a related Permanent Parliamentary Committee, and the Chairman of the Public Services Commission." In **South Africa** the "**Electoral Commission** is an independent organ and subject only to the Constitution and the law." And in the **UK**, from which Tanzania would most probably copy, the Electoral Commission is appointed by the Parliament. So, except for Kenya and probably Uganda most countries have tried to give the commissions enough freedom and power.

By the few examples provided above, it is clear that our Electoral Commission remains apart from most others. It is unique - unique in the sense that it does not possess the very important aspects of its objectives: impartiality, authority, and power; the consequences of which are deficiency and hence lack of confidence from the general public. It is obvious that such provisions in our constitution affect public perceptions about the independence, the freedom, and the credibility of the Electoral Commissions, especially when the results of the presidential elections announced by those Electoral Commissions cannot be challenged in a court of law. Many people tend to feel that the Commission is somehow biased. This is why there has been a cry for a change of the constitution of the United Republic of Tanzania. In the White Paper, Judge Kisanga's Commission realized this fact and advised the government to review it, but Mr. Mkapa was too smart to take the advice. There is no talking about free and fair elections, if we do not want to talk about changes in our Constitution. Right here, we see a problem. Some of us do not want to even think or hear about amending the Constitution. They will probably tell and convince us why; but despite my limited knowledge of Tanzanian politics, I still can read and remember our having made amendments at least seven times (1961, 1962, 1964, 1965, 1984, 1990, and 1992) and changing our constitution once in 1977. I have no idea what has happened to our fellow Tanzanians who tend to think now that our Constitution is equivalent to the commandments of God!

With or without improving the establishment of the Electoral Commission, its mechanics and performance need even more attention. We have had a good number of elections since independence; but for the sake of our analysis, let us only concentrate on the two general elections (2000 and 1995) and only refer once in a while to the other past elections. This is for the simple reason that these are the times when general election involved multiparty opposition.

On the morning of Sunday, October 29th 1995, over 6.8 million voters (about 77% of all registered voters) countrywide exercised their constitutional rights to choose the persons they wanted as their leaders under the new multiparty system. As it would be expected, there were problems just from the word go: some obvious, some not. Starting with the obvious, there were reports about double-registration, underage registration, shortened registration period, selective extension of the registration period in some areas, foreign registration, "importation" of people from the mainland to register in the islands of Zanzibar, media showing favoritism to the ruling party, and the delay of voting facilities and officers in many stations of Zanzibar and Dar es Salaam that necessitated re-elections in Dar es salaam on November 19th.

Although these may have been caused by very genuine reasons, there are still echoes of complaints even now and it is more of a problem to leave the complaints unattended and assume that all is well. Opposition leaders felt that the entire process was incorrect and demanded that the NEC nullify the elections nationwide. Their demand was disregarded. They then boycotted the re-election in Dar es Salaam. And on the other hand, immediately after the election, the Civic United Front (CUF) representatives protested against Dr. Salmin's victory. They declined attending the Parliament as a sign of refusal to recognize the legitimacy of Dr. Salmin Amour as the president of Zanzibar because, they claimed, there were forgeries/frauds. One of the not so obvious problems is the claim by CUF that CCM stole votes. Up till today some people, especially CUF members believe that their candidate, Sheikh Seif Sharrif Hamad won the presidency race that year. However, to their surprise, Dr. Salmin was announced the winner by a very simple majority. He won by 50.5%: the victory of 1,565 votes out of a total of 328,977. There was a real problem here, and the problem was well defined by the international observers who reported a number of shortcomings during the process.

The international observers made a good number of valid and logical observations. Most of these observations would substantially help to improve our elections. It would be wise for us to consider them in depth; but ironically we neglect them. The following are some of the observations and recommendations made by the SADC PARLIAMENTRY FORUM:

Arising from its work, the SADC Parliamentary Forum Observer Mission made the following general observations:

- It was commendable that women formed a significant proportion of the electoral staff and voters.
- The elections on the mainland generally took place in a peaceful manner in contrast to Zanzibar where violence, intimidation, excessive use of force by the police and organisational deficiencies were widespread.
- One of the major features of the Tanzanian electoral environment was the constitutional provisions related to the unilateral character of the appointment (and dismissal) of the members of the National Electoral Commission (NEC) and the Zanzibar Electoral Commission (ZEC) by the respective Presidents of Tanzania and Zanzibar.
- In addition, the electoral laws of both parts of the United Republic provide that the decision on the results of the presidential elections in mainland Tanzania and Zanzibar by those electoral commissions cannot be challenged in a court of law. These laws also govern the payment of a relatively large sum as deposit for the lodging of election petitions in parliamentary elections.
- There were a number of allegations of irregularity regarding the registration. These included double-registration, underage registration, shortness of the registration period, selective extension of the registration period in some areas, foreign registration and "importation" of people from the mainland to register in the islands of Zanzibar. We were unfortunately not in

a position to satisfactorily investigate these allegations. We noted, however, that the lack of a national identification system made it possible for some irregularities.
- As far as the campaign is concerned, we observed that the CCM was clearly far better resourced than the opposition parties, and that the media, and particularly the state owned press and broadcasters, favored the ruling party. There was no level playing field as far as access to resources and the official media were concerned.
- On 29 October, the NEC conducted the poll and the count in a competent and professional manner whereas the ZEC's capacity to organize and manage the elections fell far short of expectations.
- Tanzania is one of the two unique countries in SADC that has a pre-set data for elections to be conducted.

Recommendations

Arising from the above general observations the SADC Parliamentary Forum Observer Mission had the following recommendations to make designed to improve the Tanzania electoral system and process and to entrench multi-party politics and a democratic culture:
- Tanzanian politicians should consider designing inclusive and representative procedures for the appointment (and dismissal) of the Electoral Commission as this would improve its independence, impartiality and objectivity;
- The NEC should use its legal powers effectively to direct state owned media to give equal opportunities to all political parties and candidates contesting the elections;
- All parties should have equal access to public resources for campaigning, to ensure a level playing field;
- Measures should be put in place to eliminate excessive use of force by the police against the population and those police agents who use brutality against the population should be brought to court;
- Provisions should be made to enable aggrieved parties to challenge the decisions of the electoral commission regarding registration, delimitation of electoral boundaries, the election results or any other relevant matters;
- The electoral authorities should provide political parties, candidates, voters and any other interested persons with the opportunity to inspect the voters' register and make appropriate objections to correct the register before the election day;
- The government should introduce a reliable national identification system, as this would improve the conduct of registration and

polling;
- Voter education should be carried out throughout the various phases of the electoral process, by the electoral commission, political parties, civil society groups and the churches, in order to encourage high levels of political participation by the voters, and a better understanding of voting procedures and the rights and obligations of the citizens;
- The electoral authorities, key political actors from both the ruling party and the opposition, representatives of the media, the police and other role-players should be able to dialogue and address problems, even during the divisive electoral campaign. The electoral authorities should set up such regular meetings; and
- An up to date census should be used as a basis for the registration of voters. The last census in Tanzania was carried out in 1980. By SADC PARLIAMENTRY FORUM, International Observers in the 1995 General Elections in Tanzania.

Unlike 1995, the election in 2000 in the mainland was much better in comparison; but most of the problems still persisted, one being the same formation of the electoral commission. Most other problems also re-occurred and the international observers made almost the same observations and recommendations. In contrast, in Zanzibar the experience was much worse. This time it went to another level of killings by the police forces. Both the experiences have made our country's international reputation suffer significantly. In 1995, Zanzibar resulted in losing merits to receive aid from international donors. In 2000 the experience was translated as abuse of human rights and had a severe impact internationally.

Parliament

Chapter three (3) of section three (3) of the Constitution of the United Republic of Tanzania (1977) contains Articles that provide for the establishment, composition, and functions of the Parliament. This is one of the three branches of our country's administration that takes part in checks-and-balances (separation of power) of political leadership in order to avoid any possibility of tyranny. The major responsibility of the Legislative Branch is to make and write laws that regulate and control the conduct of the government and the general public. Comprised of representatives from every constituency, the Parliament should be an independent branch that works interdependently with the other two branches: the executive, and the judiciary.

Just as in education system, our political system was modeled after the British system. Before independence the legislative council, and later, the national assembly was under the queen of England. The Tanzanian political system is modeled after the British system in the sense of having the parliamentary system in which the executive is constitutionally answerable to the Parliament as opposed to the presidential system which operates under stricter separation of powers. Our national assembly structure is, however, by far different from the bicameral structure of the UK Parliament that comprises the upper house (House of Lords) and the lower house (House of Commons).

Since early sixties our parliament has grown through a number of changes in terms of laws, size, and number of representation, the major one, being that of 1992 after re-introduction of multipartyism, but its legislative role has remained largely the same.

To assume its responsibilities effectively the national assembly in a multiparty system needs to have equal proportionality of representation. The tables below show the current distribution of representation.

Table 4: Distribution of Parliamentary Representation 2000 General Election

Party	Const. Members	Special Seat	Pres. Nominee	Hse. of Repres.	Att. General	Tot.	%ge
CCM	199	40	9	5	1	254	86.1
CUF	17	4	1	0	0	22	7.46
CHADEMA	4	1	0	0	0	5	1.69
TLP	4	1	0	0	0	5	1.69
UDP	1	1	0	0	0	2	0.68
Required Strength	231	48	10	5	1	295	
Vacant Seats	6	1	0	0	0	7	

Table 5: Distribution of Parliamentary Representation After 2005 General Election

Party	Const. Members	Special Seat	Pres. Nominee	Hse. of Repres.	Att. General	Tot.	%ge
CCM	206	59	6	3	1	275	85.14
CUF	19	10	0	2	0	31	9.6
CHADEMA	5	6	0	0	0	11	3.41
TLP	1	0	0	0	0	1	0.31
UDP	1	0	0	0	0	1	0.31
Required Strength	232	75	6	5	1	319	98.76
Vacant Seats	0	0	4	0	0	4	1.24

This distribution offers a very clear picture of the ineffectiveness of our legislative branch. It is evident that with a structure of almost one political party (ruling) taking over 85% of the seats, there can yet be any real input from the opposition, especially on matters decided by votes, which unfortunately are most crucial. The challenge goes back to the opposition to regulate the proportionality of representation because it is through their agenda that they will have better representation in the Parliament. It is the responsibility of each party to aim at increasing their representation in the parliament. Otherwise, it is also the responsibility of each member to realize that they are elected by the people for national interest and not for the political parties. They should then represent the people fairly and rightly despite the prevailing situation because everything grows and develops with time – our multiparty system is at its infant stage but will grow as we nurture it.

Back to the time prior to multipartyism, our parliament had 100% one party representation but with more meaningful challenge to the government than does the current composition. In the current situation decisions tend to be of best interest to the party with majority members than to the nation's best interest.

The legislative branch is also charged with another distinguished task, which is unquestionably of high importance in the political framework of our country. That is the role of endorsing the presidential nominees for high political positions, which is probably the most important aspect of checks and balances. The process now allows the Parliament a very brief interval to make such an important decision of confirmation of nominees. Nominees are normally confirmed shortly, sometimes within a few hours, after the names are read in the Parliament leaving just a small window for evaluation of previous records of performance of the individuals in question. This is not enough time to have effective voting by the members, and therefore the Parliament is currently mostly being used purely as nothing more than a rubber stamp thereby corrupting the very core feature of its function. This is a serious deficiency in our political system. Checking the powers of the executive branch is among the key roles of the legislature. This is too far a significant task to be accomplished within hours. Through the parliamentary commissions, the legislative branch needs enough time to seek information and pursue an understanding necessary for making its decision on the suitability of the person in question. The time span may vary depending on the position or agenda on the table but at least members of the legislature should be given enough time to accomplish things satisfactorily. In my opinion, for effective confirmation the Parliament should require a specified minimum number of days in which to review career and professional records of each individual to be confirmed before making its decision on the suitability of each person in question. The Parliament should require at least two weeks from the time a nominee's name is mentioned to the time of confirmatory voting in which to review these records. This review should include among other things questioning the nominees, followed by evaluation of the ethical and moral standards of the nominees. This procedure would help Parliamentary voters to gain an understanding of a person they are about to vote for or against and would add to the effectiveness of each vote. This may seem like an irksome and unnecessary process but its authenticity and usefulness will strengthen our political system in the future.

Government
The government is the executive branch of the three branches of administration. It is the sovereign. The government of our country is headed by the President who is the chief executive and the commander-in-chief of the defense forces. The government also is comprised of the ministries and other central and local government entities. There is the Vice President and the President of Zanzibar assisting him. There is also the Prime Minister and the cabinet, which includes, among other members, the Attorney General.

The structure of government has not changed much since indepedence. There have been some minor changes here and there in some positions; but the same structure has been maintained. We have, for instance, had positions of First Vice President, Prime Minister and second Vice President, and Deputy Prime Minister in a few cases. Of course the concern here is not really the structure but rather the efficiency and harmony with which governance is carried-out, its performance and competence.

Most of our economic problems are closely associated with the performance of this branch especially in times of centralization of most sectors when the state owned all means of production. In the first two decades of our union, the government was the main employer. Therefore many things depended on the performance and efficiency of the government. But by early 1980, the situation proved that Tanzanians could not have dependency on the government wholly and develop economically. This is when we found ourselves in ambiguity because the realities of socialism turned out to be so harsh to us; yet we wanted to maintain our Ujamaa, at least theoretically, but also wanted to introduce into the same social spectrum, "the capitalist private-profit system." As I wrote earlier, the second and third phases, having realized the problem of unaccountability and bureaucracy, tried to decentralize many sectors and have the executive branch carrying out the governance. The aim here, was to enhance production. There are recorded improvements but there is still a lot to be done.

Police Force

Quality performance by our police force is still very questionable. The size of the force is still very insufficient to combat the increasing crimes of the growing population of our country. By 2004 Tanzania had the police-citizens ratio of 1:1,300 as per URT. The technology used is decrepit and outdated. Worse still is the problem of corruption in this important department of the government, especially the very obvious one in the traffic department that provides incentive for the criminals to do their evil acts. In this area, we need to accept failures so that we can start anew. In order to provide the Tanzanian people with security and safety of life we definitely need to professionalize our police force and make it capable of handling the complexities of modern society. Alongside with the judiciary, the police force should be prepared to face the changes that are brought by political and social development. There are going to be more and more complicated issues of crimes and many evils and we need to prepare for this. The present situation can give us a glimpse of what I am actually referring to, because if we visit the courts records, we realize that there is an alarming increase in the number of reported crimes. In 1995 there were 2,493 criminal cases in high court and the number grew up to 3,184 in the year (2004). There were 3,292 civil claims in 1995 which grew to 5,291 in 2004. In primary courts there were a total 29,380 cases in 1995. The same grew to 43,228 in 2004. The civil claims were 8,313 and 10,140 in the respective years. (Source: High Court)

Again the point here is less of numbers than it is of the complexities of the problems and the crimes. Morals are worsening day after day, while technology gives people ways to communicate and manipulate things easily. Serial killing, bank robberies, white-collar crimes, cyber crimes and other organized crimes are growing in both magnitude and complexity. No doubts we need a more capable force to match these crimes.

As already discussed earlier, and as evidenced by the present political and social situation, changes are happening rapidly. Governments need to prepare to go with the pace. To a greater magnitude, we have a job to do in order to modernize our police force. I mentioned earlier that crime is growing with technology. Due to the advancement of technology, communication between people or groups of people in different parts of the world is quick, easy and sometimes free; plans of travel and movements between places can also be made in an instant. People can be highly mobile on this village earth. We are advocating unity with other African nations; this is an excellent agenda towards economy liberalization; but issues of security and safety of citizens should be of paramount importance. So as we strive to build the economy, it is significant that security of the people be given deserving priority. A very noble purpose, our generosity to refugees from Rwanda and Uganda had costed our people a fortune on the lake-zone regions. East African unity seems again to be a threat after a possibility of free movement within these countries. There is obviously no nation can put generosity over the security of its people. We therefore need to make sure that the security the Tanzanian people becomes a priority.

Army (Tanzania People's Defense Forces)
When we mention TPDF, we remember such names as Mirisho Sarakikya, the late Abdallah Twalipo, David Lubozi Msuguri, Ernest Mwita Kyaro, Robert Philemon Mboma, George Waitara, Gideon Sayore, Tumainiel Kiwelu, Martin Mwakalindile and many others who served our nation with great loyalty and patriotism. These are the men who led our army as Chiefs of Defense Forces (CDF's) and Chiefs of Staff at different times of the 50-year-stretch-history of our nation.

These men, among others, have protected our borders and kept our freedom and peace. These are the men that worked tirelessly in 1978 to get Idd Amin Dada out of our land and Uganda. These are the men that did not hesitate to cross our borders to bring hope whenever there was a cry of freedom elsewhere in the South, North or West.

During these five decades we have lost a good number of our men and women in other countries as the sacrifice we gave for the freedom of fellow African brothers and sisters in the continent. These are heroes that died in the line of duty to redeem fellow human beings from oppression. We have gained a good reputation because of our involvement to free others.

The history of TPDF began concurrently with the history of our union back in 1964. At that time we had an army of few thousand officers (about 3000) with a few old fashioned World War II rifles. Today, our country has a gigantic army of men and women equipped with modern weapons and machines.

Mkapa's administration has been accused sometimes for over expenditure in TPDF. Some people believe that since our nation is peaceful and on good terms with neighbors, we should not spend as much in the army. This is a wrong way of thinking and there is a colossal misunderstanding of what it takes to maintain a nation's security.

Nobody knew we were going to war with Uganda in 1978. Nobody knows what will happen to the borders of our nation when the morrow comes. It is precisely during times of peace that we have to strengthen our forces. Bible readers have observed that "it wasn't raining when Noah built the ark". He was prepared before. We cannot wait until war breaks out before we reinforce our defense forces. It is good that the Mkapa's administration realized this fact and did a good job. This job of strengthening our forces should continue in the next administration. The world is unpredictable. We should have a strong army.

Nevertheless, TPDF has recently been accused of the shocking events of recurring explosion of expired bombs in TPDF camps near residential areas in the city Dar es Salaam. It first happened in Mbagala in May 2009 when one late afternoon explosions erupted from a storage shed, catching people off-guard. Chaos abounded, people trying to run from and to every direction without proper knowledge of exactly what was at stake. Lives and properties were lost or badly damaged.

The government denied full responsibility of the explosions, by an explanation that it was the people who followed the bombs by moving to the excluded area. Although the government might have been liable to the big question of who should have been responsible with protecting its reserved area from being invaded; and what legal actions were ever taken against trespassers.

Nonetheless, the government compensated the victims; but complaints were heard from the victims about the meager compensation. Most people still complain about the amount that could neither rebuild nor repair the badly damaged homes of the victims. To the general public this appeared to be one of the careless incidents that marred the keenness of fourth phase administration. A popular demand came up that the Minister responsible should resign; but the minister did not resign because there was no error in judgment or act that would connect him directly to the events.

After such an awful incident, most Tanzanians believed that the government would have learnt a lesson and would do whatever it takes to prevent such occurrences in the future. Sadly, just about one and a half years later, in February 2011, similar explosions occurred in another TPDF camp at Gongolamboto within the same city of Dar es Salaam. This time it was at night when explosions began and people over found themselves in a similar chaotic situation. Likewise lives and properties were lost and the government did the same thing, offering little compensation, explanation or justification.

Judiciary

The judiciary branch functions under chapter five (5) of section four (4) of the Tanzanian Constitution. Our judiciary system structure has the court of appeal of Tanzania (CAT), established on 15th August, 1979, and was inaugurated by President Julius K. Nyerere on 22nd October, 1979; and is presently comprised of 15 judges (including the Chief Justice, CJ – Jaji Mkuu); High court with 58 judges (including the Principal Judge, PJ – Jaji Kiongozi) distributed in 15 zones, regional magistrate courts with 108 judges by 2011, district courts and about 653 primary courts. The chief role of the judiciary branch is to translate the law.

At this infant stage of democracy in Tanzania, this branch assumes a vital responsibility; but our judiciary system has a lot of irregularities and imperfections in its methods of carrying out functions and duties. It is said that there is still a colossal possibility of manipulation by influential people. This means we have to work hard, just like in other sectors, to improve our judicial system too. What must be pointed out here is that our judicial system leaves a lot to be desired in the stance of justice in the nation. Tanzanian citizens deserve the best of an impartial judicial system. Disappointingly, not much has been done in building up a powerful law-enforcement system in the nation. An impotent law-enforcement system remains to be the only substitute. This is no accident. It is the effort of the Executive branch to manipulate and play with the checks-and-balance branches of the nation so as to remain unchecked.

Judge Vincent Lyimo, on his retirement day, the 14th Sept 2011, expressed his feelings by saying that the government provides surplus funding to the parliament while the judiciary suffers great shortage. He went on saying that there hasn't been a day when the parliamentary sitting was ever postponed or cancelled due to lack of funds. Similarly on the executive branch, no single presidential trip with the usual large convoys has ever been cancelled or postponed on the grounds of shortage of funds. President Kikwete has actually been accused of too many foreign trips, making more trips than any of his forerunners.

But the Judiciary suffers great shortage of funds to an extent of putting aside many of its cases. Many other judicial activities are either impeded or unmet due to funding. Cases take too long before judgments are rendered. Shortage of workers with low salaries is what exists in our judiciary. Financial and material resources are also a big problem in this important branch of checks-and-balances. This weakens our judicial system badly and corruption obviously finds its way easily into the system.

On the other hand, though, the Executive and the Legislative branches continue to enjoy surplus funding: brand new luxurious SUV's; handsome packages are what the members enjoy regardless of the nation's economic status while the judiciary, which is charged with provision of justice has by far less resources than needed! In the recent past, getting into the parliament has become a very lucrative endeavor.

Our courts are now still dealing with small and medium level legal problems among individuals and/or institutions. But as more and more citizens become aware of their rights as human beings and as citizens; and as freedom of choice and of speech grows; and when political parties become stronger and demand democracy more vigorously and when more groups of fundamentalists, activists, revolutionists, extremists, conservatives, futuristics and fanatics will prevail our citizens will have more lines dividing them and our courts will be dealing with more complicated civil and legal problems that bring division among people with respect to their values and ideologies.

This conclusion is not predicting trouble in our nation, but it tells the reality. In 1961 we dealt with about 10 million people. Today we are dealing with about 40m people, a population increase of 300% for 50 years. With the same increase rate we shall have more than 160 million people to deal with by 2061. Or by the current average annual growth rate, we will still have over 100 million people to deal with. Society issues will also increase by both magnitude and complexity. This is a situation that requires realization of the need to prepare a perfect legal system.

In other nations, choice of leaders no longer depends only on the academic, professional or career qualifications of individuals, but to a further consideration of their ideologies, values, and their stand on social issues. Moral, ideological, and many other day-to-day issues have become an effective part of political activities and decisions, and these issues are dividing people significantly.

In such situations more fundamental differences among people of different ideologies and beliefs come out openly and the judiciary takes a key role in regulating these issues for the best interest of the nation. As I suggested in my discussion of the police force, this is another important area that needs long-term preparation to face the complexities of modern society. As I also mentioned in my discussion of the role and mechanism of the electoral commission, impartiality and independence of the judicial system, like in the electoral commission, are key aspects. That again pulls us to the powers of the president in an effective system of checks and balances.

As per our current Constitution, the President plainly appoints judges. There is no confirmation from the Parliament or any governmental segment. There is a risk that we face of having our judiciary branch to become just an extension of the executive branch addition; by having appointments that just suit the best interest of the appointing authority and that is a serious risk we face as a nation.

Although our opposition parties' leaders seem to be getting more and more comfortable with the Constitution, a proposal to review our Constitution was and still is a legitimate and a noble proposal.

As I have mentioned in preceding paragraphs, I believe corruption to be one of our country's biggest problems. Like HIV/AIDS, corruption is a multi-sectoral problem. The judiciary is expected to contribute significantly in the war against corruption. However, the system is still very vulnerable and itself very prone to corruption. There is obvious corruption in our courts – so obvious it is almost like a part of the employment contract. This makes the court system to be exactly what it was intended not to be.

7

The New Era

With the foregoing analysis, one thing is obvious at this point, and that is: we are no longer going to The Promised Land. Fifty years have gone by - there is no sign of getting the fruits of socialism. Instead, recent years have been characterized by an increased gulf between the lower and the upper classes. It is imperative that we make a subtle shift of viewpoint and face the reality and start practicing what we preach.

Someone once said, "Someday everyone will carry his own burden." referring to the shift in political ideology from socialism to capitalism. Many Tanzanians were enraged for what seemed to undermine the principles of Ujamaa. We were so naïve and could hardly comprehend how someone could dare advocate such a capitalist thought in a country so faithful to socialistic theories. We refused to accept the bitter fact that there comes a time when we really have to carry our burden individually. Now reality has hit us. That was the truth, if only our leaders knew as much and acted accordingly, perhaps we would still be on course, en route to the Promised Land.

In spite of the vision and commitment our founding father, Mwalimu Julius Nyerere, the ideals of Ujamaa have not been realized. The leaders that followed have attempted to pursue a closely-related agenda, but with no success. And herein lies the main task for the incumbent administration, i.e., to redefine our national goals, expound on our policies and work implementable action plans.

In conclusion, the three phases of our administration can be credited for the following major achievements: the first phase under Mwalimu Nyerere unified our people under Ujamaa and thus established a peaceful society. Although its vision reflected in the spirit of Ujamaa policy never took off the ground, it set and established a vision and direction for the future. The second phase changed the hypothetical economic agenda to an open market approach, although of course, the changes had many shortcomings with it, especially the discipline that is necessary for the implementation of policies. The third phase endeavored to implement the adjustment programs with some degree of discipline. They tried to eradicate socio-economic issues that hindered economic growth such as tax evasion, corruption, unaccountability, indiscipline in productivity, and lack of work ethic. There are complaints though, that this administration concentrated too much on governmental issues and neglected the public. Indeed the third phase of administration took an important step to repair the utterly battered economy. Yet, the reform has remained, to a great extent, uneven and inconsistent.

Goran Hyden, a Professor of Political Science at the University of Florida in USA, and once a political science professor at USDM (1971 - 1977), gives his opinion on the history of Tanzanian leadership and political power history as follows:

"If the Nyerere years were a blind race toward a false paradise and the Mwinyi period a chaotic free-for-all dance in the rediscovered marketplace, the past ten years under the country's third President have been an attempt at a more disciplined march toward specific policy goals. The discipline in the ranks still leaves a lot to be desired, but despite these weaknesses there is growing agreement that Tanzania is slowly being integrated into the global economy with all the costs and benefits associated with such integration. This process has begun at the apex of the system with reforms of public finance and administration. It has trickled into the economy as a whole in the form of a relatively stable currency, acceptable level of inflation, and a stronger emphasis on pushing development funds to district and local levels as part of a new National Growth and Poverty Reduction Strategy. The majority of Tanzanians, however, are still to experience the full benefits of these reforms. It is no surprise, therefore, that the public continues to lament the cost of living and other shortcomings, not the least corruption, poor service delivery and infra-structural maintenance that continue to adversely affect the image of the ongoing reform programs. The local media are full of such complaints every day."

The Kikwete Presidency

Jakaya M. Kikwete- The 4th President of Tanzania

The 2005 General Elections and peaceful transition from the third phase to the current have earned international recognition for the manner in which it was conducted. Elections were planned well and peacefully and were coordinated with efficiency seldom seen in Africa. We demonstrated to the entire world that we are a peace-loving nation, mature enough to appreciate our political differences; and according to international observers, democracy has reached a good maturity level in Tanzania.

It was, however, argued that President Kikwete's popularity then was a key factor in the 2005 smooth elections. He was so popular across the political spectrum that elections remained just as formalities. The results told the same story. Mr. Kikwete went to the State House by over 80 per cent victory as if it was a one party election. Research had indicated that Mr. Kikwete was fulfilling all the criteria of a good political candidate: political, economic, and social.

Politically, Mr. Kikwete was indisputably popular, probably more than any other person in the country then – and this might have been his crowning virtue. A commentator once said "Kikwete is in fact the most popular man in East Africa now and the second in Africa after Nelson Mandela."

Socially, he seemed to represent a broader segment of Tanzanian community. At 55, Kikwete was still considered "young" and so he was incredibly accepted by young generation, who was the majority voters, and seemed to be a representative of this group to the political power of the country. Now why he was considered young at 55 remained to be an unimportant question, at least for then.

Mr. Kikwete also knew how to well-connect himself with the older folks. Therefore he managed to be part and parcel of that important group in the decision-making of political matters.

Additionally, Kikwete seemed to also be more accepted on both parts of the union with people of all ideologies and beliefs, than probably any of his rivals. Therefore, the 2005 elections ended with a great success, a smooth ride for Mr. Kikwete. It was actually more challenging for him to obtain candidacy in his own party than getting victory on ballots against opposition parties.

H.E Kikwete was not new to the public arena. He is a Tanzanian, born in Tanzania, raised and schooled in Tanzania. As a matter of fact, he has been in public service for three of the five decades under review in this book. Born on 7 October 1950, He has spent all his academic and career life in Tanzania. He brought with him a multidimensional experience to the State House. He has worked in- and out-of uniforms as a senior army officer and as a politician in different offices and ministries for a good number of years, yet at 55 he was still strong and capable of more contribution to the nation for another set of years.

Mr. Kikwete began his career immediately after graduating with a degree concentrating in Economics from the University of Dar-es-Salaam in 1975. He joined CCM, then known as Tanzania African National Union (TANU). Kikwete underwent military training while serving as a TANU cadre and was, at one time, seconded to the Tanzania People's Defense Forces as chief political instructor at the Monduli Central Military Academy, the country's top military training institution, located in the northern Tanzanian region of Arusha, where commissioned and commanding officers are trained for leadership in all army units. He was commissioned as a lieutenant and retired as a colonel to join politics.

Road to Presidency

Mr. Kikwete's first attempt to presidency did not go beyond party level. He lost narrowly his party's nomination to Benjamin Mkapa. Many commentators believe that Mwalimu Nyerere influenced the results in favor of Mkapa. Mr. Kikwete was then appointed Minister for Foreign Affairs after accepting his party's decision unquestionably; a position he held for all the ten years of Mkapa's presidency.

As commented earlier, Mr. Kikwete's capital was his popularity that can be traced back from July 1995 when he, and his colleague, Edward Lowassa, were clumsily nicknamed Boys-II-Men. At that time people had high hopes for Mr. Edward Lowassa to go for CCM candidature; but Mr. Lowassa, either genuinely so or for another reason, initially seemed very reluctant to seek the candidacy. At the eleventh hour, the duo made a decision and flew to Dodoma.

Unfortunately Mwalimu Nyerere wasn't very much in favor of Mr. Lowassa. A head collision with Mwalimu, therefore, jeopardized Lowassa's bid. His supporters shifted to back Mr. Kikwete.

On July 22nd 1995, Mr. Kikwete won the first part of the race that included three contestants: him, Mr. Benjamin William Mkapa and Mr. David Cleopa Msuya. Mr. Kikwete ended up being the first runner-up at the final leg when one of the contestants, Mr. Msuya was removed after the first leg voting.

Kikwete later accepted to be part of Mkapa's cabinet as Minister for Foreign Affairs and patiently waited for an entire decade. During all these years his popularity was building up so incredibly and today he is sure that his waiting was not at all in vain.

In February 2005 H.E Mr. Kikwete announced officially his bid for presidency for a second trial, and in May 2005 Kikwete was ready to face another challenge, this time with every sign of success. Somehow in the process Kikwete had captured people's hearts and all the other procedures looked like formalities.

Paving his way to victory Mr. Kikwete threw away strong rivals like John S. Malecela, the party's vice-chairman (Tanzania Mainland-Tanganyika), a seasoned diplomat, politician and a former PM who seemed to believe that he had to become a Tanzanian president, for his history to be fully written; Professor Abdallah Kigoda, a minister in both the past two cabinets and very closely associated with the immediate former president, Ben Mkapa.

Others were Frederick Sumaye, the then outgoing PM who served all 10 yrs under Mkapa; Patrick Chokala (former Press Secretary to the President); Idd Simba (Former Minister for Trade and Industries); Ali Karume, and John Shibuda.

In the second part of the race, Mr. Kikwete battled it out with seasoned politicians such as Dr. Salim Ahmed Salim, the former secretary of African Union (AU) previously known as Organization of African Unity (OAU) and first the Tanzanian diplomat to the United Nations.

In the race also, was Professor Mark Mwandosya, an intellectual who had gained much admiration from the Tanzanian public by then.

While Dr. Salim approached the candidacy nomination with diplomatic decency and honesty, Mark Mwandosya relied on his high integrity and the fact that he was going to be, if he would be elevated to the top office, the first Tanzanian Prof. President. But Kikwete capitalized in a perfect combination of popularity, long time preparation, and well-calculated strategy of victory.

Kikwete's long service in political activities was a huge plus. He has involved himself in political affairs since he graduated from the University of Dar es salaam back in 1975 and served as the Head of Department of Defense and Security at the very tender age of thirty years under Nyerere's administration. During the last thirty years Kikwete was duly involved in the political affairs in his party, much of which, he has been in the Central and National Executive Committees of the party.

On the other hand too, Kikwete had passed a popularity test since 1995. CCM knew since then that if they had to bring forward a winning name, Kikwete was the name that would meet more acceptance. CCM knew it had the right card.

After a very careful consideration of all the factors surrounding the country's fourth presidential race, Kikwete turned out to be the most suitable candidate. So CCM came together, made consideration of all the economic and political factors of the country and voted to make Kikwete the party's flag bearer. The rest is now history.

Below is a table summarizing results of the 2005 Presidential Election:

Name	Party	Votes	Percentage
Jakaya M. Kikwete	CCM	9,123,952	80.28
Ibrahim H. Lipumba	CUF	1,327,125	11.68
Freeman A. Mbowe	CHADEMA	668,756	5.88
Augustine L. Mrema	TLP	84,901	0.75
Edmund S. Mvungi	NCCR-MAGEUZI	55,819	0.49
Christopher Mtikila	DP	31,083	0.27
Emmanuel J. Makaidi	NLD	21,574	0.19
Anna C. Senkoro	PPT MAENDELEO	18,783	0.17
Leonard K. Shayo	MAKINI	17,070	0.15
Paul H. Kyara	SAU	16,414	0.14

But the story wasn't similarly pleasant in the 2010 General Elections. H. E. Kikwete dropped by about a 20% margin, getting only 61.17% despite having only 8 competing parties in 2010 as opposed to 10 in 2005. The race which included CCM, CHADEMA, CUF, NCCER-MAGEUZI, UDPD, TLP, and APPT-Maendeleo ended up with a lot of complaints from the opposition parties. Results from many constituents were not accepted. CHADEMA's Dr. Wilbroad Slaa was the most challenging candidate to Kikwete; and was more fiercely opposed to the presidential results. There were, in fact, rumors that CHADEMA wanted to organize a nationwide strike for the results. However, the situation calmed down after a while and things came back to normal. Below is the summary of 2010 presidential election results

Name	Party	Votes	Percentage
Jakaya M. Kikwete	CCM	5,276,827	61.17
Willbroad P. Slaa	CHADEMA	2,271,941	26.34
Ibrahim H. Lipumba	CUF	695,667	8.06
P. M. Kugwa	PPT MAENDELEO	96,933	1.12
Hashim S. Rungwe	NCCR-MAGEUZI	26,388	0.31
Muttamwega B. Mgahywa	TLP	17,482	0.20
Yahmi N. Dovutwa	UPDP	13,176	0.15

Mr. Kikwete's drop of popularity made room for greater opposition; and the opposition was from both within and without. Even his fellow CCM members were losing hope in him. Right before the general elections a team of what were believed to be CCM members planned for a new party registration by the name of CCJ. It was believed that CCJ's main goal was to make sure that Mr. Kikwete wasn't coming back to presidency for a second term. Nevertheless, the most powerful man in the nation read the signs of times and by his network did what was necessary to make sure that CCJ wasn't going to get any further; and CCJ didn't get registration on time; therefore, its mission collapsed.

This opposition within CCM gave birth to the post-election ideological divide. Groups were created within CCM. In his first bid for candidacy in 2005, Mr. Kikwete was said to have had formed a powerful network that prepared his smooth path to victory. It has been lamented that some of the powerful members in his network turned their back against him and, much as it has been very unpleasant and inconvenient for them to admit, there was strife within CCM. There were divisions. There were groups of the old folks, the pro-Nyerere folks, who were watching and were saddened by the way things were run, and there were also what was known as *"wapiganaji"* who were bitterly and openly opposed to the way the government handles the corruption scandals and misconducts; and want the corrupt individuals, popularly referred to as *"Mafisadi"*, to face the hand of the law; and there were the notorious group of "mafisadi" themselves.

At one time the party leadership came up with a buzz-word of *"Kujivua gamba"* translated in English as stripping off the old skin as a snake does at old age. In this, CCM wanted to oust those who were accused of corruption, misconduct and unethical behaviors that were costing the party. This was just partially successful because the "fisadis" had financial power and were very influential. Therefore, most of them refused to resign as directed by the party leadership.

The Igunga MP, Mr. Rostam Aziz, resigned within the time frame given by the party leadership for mafisadi to drop out. While Mr. Aziz had been mentioned on the CHADEMA's list of the Mafisadi, he had, like everyone else, denied; so it wasn't very clear if his resignation was taking responsibility as directed or it was just a convenient time for him to drop because he also was quoted as claiming that he was tired of the party's political games.

Giving a closer look, imperfections and irregularities were exceedingly evident in the 2010 General Elections. Of course, the voting process looked fine and peaceful. But as someone once said: "democracy is not in the voting but in the counting". Complaints were heard from many constituents. The opposition side complaining about the way the Electoral Commission was handling matters. Counting of votes took longer than was necessary. Votes were also believed to be rigged. A few constituent covered most papers' front page headings. These were Nyamagana – Mwanza; Segerea – Dar es Salaam and Arusha Town.

Results from these constituents were delayed and rumors went around that the results were changed in favor of the ruling party. CCM lost both Arusha and Mwanza and was also believed to have lost Segerea but rigged the votes.

Part of what dropped Kikwete's popularity was his first five years in the State House which had a mix of mystery and transparency; and his administration is said to be the most dramatic of all administrations of the past. Partly, it's because of the expansion of freedom of press. The General public, in this era, has good access to information and news. This accessibility is contributed significantly by a big number of media instruments, growth and development of technology, globalization - *free movement of people and information from one end of the world to another;* and the ascendance of internet and cell phones. But the other part is also the openness of this administration that sometimes, for political reasons or pressure, or because of the ruling party's internal strife; much information has been put out to the general public, and in some cases, more than the general public needed.

Some of the unexpected news that were put to public during the first tenure of Kikwete's Presidency included: BoT's False Payment of TShs. 133 Billion under EPA; Tanzanian Embassy in Italy mismanaging TShs. 2Billion in a construction project; Tanzania daily payment of TShs. 152 million for a fake Richmond power deal; Zanzibar in political crisis; corruption in purchase of a Radar from Great Britain; controversial President's jet; demolition of houses; Fake TICTS deal; Buzwagi, Kiwira, Tangold, Meremeta, Dowans.

These and many others found their way to the public through our dailies, news websites, blogs and phone communications.

Working with a slogan of Ari Mpya; Nguvu Mpya and Kasi Mpya, meaning new spirit; new zeal and new pace, this administration, just like Mkapa's, indicated that it was going to deal with the systematic corruption problem that has grown to be the major socio-economic problem of our nation. However it is doubtful if the administration knew what it was setting itself up to. It is unclear also if the administration had the muscle in terms of resources and legal stamina, to fight the extensive corruption problem that has turned out to be a stigma to our nation. This was proven by the numerous cases that were started, just started, but never concluded.

In a few cases we have seen people taken to court very selectively and categorically. Yet still, those cases have remained perpetual despite the President's repetitive proclamation that his administration would only take people to court when fully satisfied with proof beyond reasonable doubts that the suspects have cases to answer.

Right at the beginning of this administration, in March 2006, the Tanzanian ambassador in Rome was taken to court charged with corruption and theft of over TShs. 2B in Rome Italy, in an embassy building construction transaction. Over five years now, the case is still on despite amounting testimonies from in and outside the nation. Then came the EPA scandal in which Tanzania lost over US$131 million from the *External Payment Arrears* (EPA) account held at the Bank of Tanzania (BoT) in what was then described as "dubious payments" to 22 local companies.

This happened in the 2005/06 financial budget. A few people were sent to court; and very few were convicted. The president revoked *David Balali's* appointment as the governor of the Central Bank for being connected with the payments. David Balali died few days after his dismissal (May 16th, 2008) without a word on the scandal and was accused of everything without being given a chance to defend himself anywhere. It is said, however, that the big fish of the scandals are free on the streets.

Then came the case of abuse of power that led to loss of TShs. 11B government money against Former Cabinet Ministers, *Basil Mramba* and *Daniel Yona* and a retired Permanent Secretary to the Treasury, Mr. *Gray Mgonja*. The case is still on its proceedings. There have been many other corruption cases: Radar, Richmond, and Dowans, which still persist.

This administration needs to be unbiased and gain courage on the fight against corruption. Otherwise in the fight we may create another problem if this administration isn't taking great care in dealing with this sensitive, but most destructive problem.

The most publicized event of this administration was probably the resignation of its Prime Minister, Mr. Edward Lowassa, followed by dissolution of the entire cabinet in Feb 2007, hardly 16 months after his appointment by the President and with an over 99 pc endorsement by the parliament. Lowassa's resignation was preceded by a very unique episode in Tanzania's political history of the Mwakyembe Commission Report that investigated the scandalous Richmond Electricity contract and came up with a conclusion that the contract, which wasn't for the nation's best interest, was greatly influenced by Mr. Lowassa who was then the PM. It was proven by the commission that the company in question had no experts and capability to supply power as it was earlier indicated. This resulted in resignation of the PM and two other Ministers who were closely associated with the contract. Mr. Lowassa, however, has remained strongly opposed to the accusations, arguiring that he did everything for the nation's best interest, and that everything done by his office had the President's approval.

Edward Lowassa

Our country is now experiencing a problem of disintegration that has reduced the contribution of the general public, which to me, is a problem of social matters and a hindrance to the economic development in general because the general public is not well engaged. The third phase contributed to this disintegration due to an administration that at first focused more on political rivalry and opposition than national patriotism and unity. The gulf between the haves and have-nots is continuously on the rise.

Because of obvious mistakes, there is loss of trust by the general public. It is very critical that this mistake is corrected to build the trust and confidence of citizens. The late Nyerere realized that unity and patriotism are essential tools in building a nation's economy. Former President, Mr. Mkapa has been heard repeatedly confessing that the government is incapable of doing everything on its own. The theories of economics teach us that it is both human and non-human resources that are transformed into final goods. Therefore, the government depends on the general public in development activities.

We cannot then, afford to ignore the participation of the people. We can neither afford to underutilize this form of resource by dealing with unmotivated and unprepared people. But how would people want to be involved in what they do not benefit from? The third phase missed an important point here. It did not do enough in mobilizing support from people. A nation needs to a great extent, the participation of citizens to contribute to development activities in economic, political, and social matters. Everywhere in the world, the need for the contribution of the people is essential. There has never existed a nation with a self sufficient government in such areas as security, health, and education. Therefore, the greatest asset of any nation is a people with trust and confidence in their government. Trust and confidence are actually the parents of patriotism.

There is no patriotism if people cannot be satisfied with the level of performance and integrity of their government. Therefore the fourth phase should implement for the benefit of the people what the third phase theorized for political gains – transparency and truth. And this is an important lesson that Tanzanian leaders need to learn. The tendency of concealing information and the wrongs of the leaders that the public deserves to have access to, has been a cultural problem. Our leaders need to learn to be transparent and honest, especially in times of adversity. If there is any single Tanzanian that stood at a better position than anybody else to rebuild the unity and patriotism in our country then it was the man we recently put in the white buildings housing our state-house.

Mr. President went to that office with a victory of a one party election. It was as though there had been no opposition at all! All this signified was that people had trust in him and were ready to follow the marching orders of the president to the direction he wanted to go, considering especially the large number of registered voters in the last general election. Mr. President should have capitalized on this trust; and if Mr.

President was not going to jeopardize it, he stood a better chance of getting off with a good start.

Mr. Kikwete could influence all: young and old, men and women; his party members and opposition members; Tanganyikans (I hope this term is still politically-correct) and Zanzibaris; Christians and Muslims - one and all. With a unified people, anything is achievable; and the 2005 general election offered that proof. Therefore all Mr. President had to do was start where he was with what he had.

Mr. President was not only acceptable locally but also everywhere in this world. His introduction tour across African, Arabic, European and American countries in the months of April and May 2006 met with high admiration and appreciation from leaders and investors of other countries. I am not sure what Mr. President told his audiences in those parts but comments and ratings after his tour were amazingly high.

State of our Economy
The current state of our economy is something well known to the president. Of the fifty year history of Tanzania, Mr. Kikwete has been in higher offices for three decades. He knows our economy inside-out and he had all the means to rectify its problems. The following, is what he was expected to accomplish during his tenure in Tanzania's highest office:

Poverty
More than 35% of Tanzanians are living below the poverty line, some of them living a life, as one commentator puts it, *closest to hell*. This is obviously not good news to Mr. President, but it is what makes our country one of the most popular nations in the world with her name on every economic report of poorest countries in the world, the thing I said I have heard enough and I am tired. Mr. President went to State House on the platform of better life to all Tanzanians and with a promise of a 'living wage'. But civil servants are still extremely dissatisfied with the low wages. The value of a shilling is down with an exponential fall while salary increments are limited to very low rates.

The poverty reduction strategy that has been set up should be improved and implemented sufficiently to practically reduce poverty.

Our big and obvious problem is inconsistency and imbalance in economic development. Some areas of our economy are in very good shape, some are not. Uncoordinated efforts in economic activities have been the major cause. Many reforms, strategies, and policies have been adopted during the past four decades, especially the last decade. Because of this, there have been significant economic and social developments in some areas, e.g. collection of government revenues; control of inflation, better managed government Budget, increased foreign investments, etc. But poverty has increased tremendously.

In the regions, there is an imbalance of economic development from place to place. Mr. President finished the election campaign not long ago, and later went for the thanksgiving tour. He traveled across Tanzania. He was then more informed of the state of development of our country and the differences of the same from place to place now probably more than ever before. This situation has caused people to even refuse to get transfers to other places of the country due to lagging-behind of development. Most people are not ready to work out of Dar-es-salaam, Mwanza, and Arusha, because they just cannot imagine themselves in those areas. This is obviously a problem that impacts our economic development.

Corruption

If I were to mention the worst single problem of this country, it would obviously be corruption. Corruption seems to be prevalent in all phases. The rhetoric approaches and a barking-dog style have yielded no good outcomes. The Anti-corruption Squad of the late 1970's and the Prevention and Combating of Corruption Bureau (PCCB), previously Prevention for Corruption Bureau (PCB), practiced exactly what they were meant to prevent. Therefore corruption still remains to be the most destructive yet the most accepted offense. People are committing it with all their teeth out - smiling. But it has definitely hindered the growth of our economy.

Corruption takes place at a substantial cost to our economy and adds significant vulnerability to common Tanzanian life. Corruption short-circuits our endeavors to improve economy and results in disintegrated and uncoordinated efforts which seem like filling water in a bottomless bucket. Tanzania is definitely a rich country. Tanzanians can definitely live a good life if we could take good care of our resources and our assets.

Once again a loud cry of help is made to Mr. President. Those who governed our affairs in the past made promises of fighting corruption. But corruption remains to be the oldest and the worst enemy of our economy. Now, Mr. Kikwete can, if he is willing, actually do what others pretended to do.

Agriculture

It is realized that our agriculture has been left behind. If agriculture employs more than three quarters of the present rural population; if agriculture contributes more than a half of the average total export volume; and if it is the major contributor to the nation's GDP, we obviously need to reconsider our priorities with all seriousness, Mr. President. Agriculture is the mainstream of our economy, but it has remained at micro levels. Our agriculture needs to be commercialized, professionalized, and modernized.

We need affirmative action in this sector so as to promote agriculture and all agro-related activities. The Ministry of Agriculture should be strengthened by a proper manpower, expertise, and a better budget allocation. Agriculture should be subsidized sufficiently. Investors should be encouraged to invest in agriculture. Long term plans should be developed to have farmers contribute to National Social Security Fund (NSSF) for better and long term retirement benefits, which will make it a fully-fledged employment and attract more people. Our agriculture training institutions should be equipped to prepare people who will be actively involved in a modern farming. Infrastructure and machinery in agriculture should be modernized.

Social Services (Health Care, Education, and Employment)

Social services are still in bad shape, probably worsening. Health care for the lower class is a big problem. Epidemics have been cover stories in our locals lately. We definitely need to increase promotion of preventive methods. Medical insurances should be affordable to all people. Alternative methods should be in place for those who can genuinely not afford to pay for medical care. And this should be implemented with seriousness. In times past promises were made of helping those who could not afford education and health; but reality revealed a betrayal.

Some of our problems are as old as our indepemndence. In the 1960's, we declared war against our worst enemies (ignorance, diseases, and poverty). Today, five decades down the road, ignorance is diminishing significantly; diseases and poverty are growing terribly. We again need to announce war here. We need to fight diseases and poverty as strongly as we fought against ignorance.

There has been a huge and rapid expansion in education. Changes are happening in very quick succession. A subsequent risk falls on having low-quality professionals who do not meet adequate standards and who cannot perform competently. Quality should be emphasized in our education system, probably as much as in the other sectors, too. Very close supervision of private and public education should be maintained for this is the area that holds our future as individuals and as a nation. This agrees well with section 1.2.4 of "Vision 2025" of having a well educated and learned society. A learned society is an indispensable prerequisite for development. Nations have developed without one or two of the other aspects of development such as good governance, a good political system, and natural resources; but no nation can develop without a learned people. To achieve this we need to monitor so well the degree of quality in our education system.

I would also strongly suggest deliberate plans and interest in the area of technology. We have done so well at the receiving end of science and technology. This is why a debate of whether we use Kiswahili as a medium of instruction is weakened by our scientific terminology because we have received these things from others. Time has come to have something to offer to our people and to the world. We need to strongly encourage science and technology. India and many other countries in South and East Asia have gained economic power through technology, especially the area of Information Technology (IT). This is again in tune with the shifting of the economy drivers. The world moved from an agricultural economy to an industrial economy and now the 21st century is considered to be technology-oriented.

I have discussed employment at length. What should be emphasized is that the open market approach of economy we are taking should be for the good of the nation and the citizens. Privatization and the free market economy should not be a club to punish the citizens.

Electoral Commissions
Irregularities in political activities are weakening our peace and stability. As discussed at length and suggested earlier, I think we need to review the establishment of our electoral commission. Many people have raised a concern on this issue; but it has never found its way to the opinion of the policy makers. This has especially been an issue in the third phase government. My opinion is that the fourth phase government should look into this matter with more priority and honesty. In spite of minimum complaints in the 2005 general elections and a record of significant progress, there were still complaints in the 2010 general elections; and I think we still have room for improvement in this area.

Another issue in our political system, though it may not be very obvious to some of us, whose significance to the future leadership of this nation demands attention, and that is the powers of the president. In my earlier paragraphs I made a mention of some of the officials that are nominated by the president. It seems as if the president nominates everybody! This is evidently lethal to the effectiveness of the checks and balances of the three branches of administration.

Again, there is something we need to check out here so we balance the power equation. As we grow in democracy, it is imperative that we reduce this absolute power tradition and use more efficiently the checks and balances system and elect leaders by votes. We need to reduce the number of officials nominated by the president and elect more leaders by votes. I hold firmly the belief that this will enhance accountability and reliability.

Security

Security is another important area that needs a comprehensive review. An opinion has been formed in some developed countries that security is the fourth among human basic needs. I tend to concur with opinion because food, shelter and clothing make sense only when we are secure and peaceful. The weakest link in our security and legal system is the inability of law enforcement. It is evidently clear that if there is no law enforcement our security is at high risk no matter how many laws are in place. Just a few months after the new government was in power, we had heard more than a few occasions of serious robberies of multiple-millions of shillings and brutal deaths. This is an alarming situation. It is as if we want to get to the survival for the fittest rule of the jungle. Those who are more powerful, survive: those who are not, perish!

Therefore, without running the risk of repetition, I would suggest we need to modernize and professionalize all the sectors dealing with the security and safety of the citizens, especially the police force. It is also important, for the fourth phase government to look into forces behind the lack of security to our people: poverty, unemployment, and injustice. These problems may prompt a cold war on the dissatisfied section and hence lead to an acceleration of crimes.

This area needs a very broad and comprehensive long-term plan of improvement. But we have no choice. It is obvious that there is a great weakness somewhere in our security network and we need to do our responsibility. We need to keep up with the security issues in the nation.

Women and Youth

Active engagement of youth and women in decision-making positions is a very important criterion of today's social and political development. A "woman's position" has especially become a central issue on the global economic and political development. Our country has, especially the third government, made reasonable progress in the area of empowering women. But we still need to do much more than we have done. The percentage of women in schools, colleges, and key leadership positions should be improved by far. The statistics indicate that the percentage of women representation in the parliament has increased from 15% (1995) to 22.5% (2004) and the percentage of women in the last cabinet was about 15% from 11% in 1995. In higher learning institutions the percentage of women still falls far below 35%. We can do better. These percentages should be at 51%! At least that's what the population ratio suggests. Mr. President saw this and promised to have more women in the cabinet. The recent cabinet selection has proven his statement. By percentile scale there was no increase in full ministers' positions, but generally speaking the percentage is somewhere above 21%. That is another step in a good direction.

Tanzania has a very good reserve of female manpower. We have fine leaders in women and we need to utilize their abilities. People like the Former Director of United Nations Human Settlement Program (HABITAT) Professor Anna Kajumulo Tibaijuka, the first President of the African Parliament, Mrs. Gertrude Mongela, and many other leaders like Tabitha Siwale, Lucy Lameck, Anna Makinda, Fatma Said Ali and Anna Abdallah, have given a tremendous contribution to the nation through their long and honorable service. And the leaders of new generation like Mary Nagu, Zakhia Meghji, Mauwa Daftari, Rita Mlaki, Shamim Khan, Tatu Ntimzi, Dr. Asha-Rose Migiro have also made important contributions with their leadership abilities and have proven by far that the only thing women of our country have less than men is opportunity.

Inclusion of more women in the cabinet and other positions is a powerful gesture the president gave to the little girls of our nation: an indication to a little Tanzanian girl that she has a meaningful role in her society. Mr. President has put another block on the foundation wall of change. The change from the old notion our society has embraced for centuries that little girls cannot grow up to have any meaningful role in a society. This has caused denial of opportunities to Tanzanian women and is in any case completely against human rights. Mr. President deserves credit here for steering such a revolution, although of course Mr. President had to conveniently enlarge the cabinet so that he can have both a bigger number of women without loss of many men, but at least it makes sense. But that quite frankly generates another concern on the powers of the president on the national issues. It was not until the creation of the new cabinet when most people realized that the president can alter the structure of the cabinet as he pleases including forming ministries that have a single department to oversee and have a one line organization structure from the top of the ministry to the bottom of the department. Is it time for the public to know every single cent of the taxpayers' money that is channeled to the expenses of the cabinet?

While women are now being elevated to the higher positions, youth have been left out of the equation of power. We need more youth in national affairs. The world has a new agenda. Fresh minds are needed to run the country. Tanzania has been adequately contented with the contribution of the older folks and we need to appreciate the way these guys have brought us thus far. But it is time for a change. It is time to try out new brains. We need to utilize the investments we have put into our youth. By youth I mean young, energetic, intelligent and educated people who have the guts and the power to change our country. We have these people. All they need is opportunity. Mr. President: afford them the opportunity. Try them out.

When Nyerere took presidency of this country, he had but very few professionals to use as leaders and therefore a few of them were to be circulated on different positions of the cabinet no matter what. The very surprising thing today is: five decades down the road and after a population increase of 300% we still want to maintain some of these folks who served during Nyerere's era! Something is obviously not right. Otherwise we should have prepared a new generation of leadership because the Nyerere guys have finished their part.

Lastly, Mr. President will undoubtedly agree with this brief analysis that the account of our fifty year journey is not impressive. After forty years, the Israelites arrived to the Promised Land; after fifty years, Tanzanians are nowhere near the Promised Land. Where are we going?

Bibliography

Bovard, James. Attention Deficit Democracy, Palgrave Macmillan, 2005.

Carson, B. M.D with Cecil Murphey. Think Big, Zondervan, 1992.

Covey, Stephen R. The 7 Habits of Highly Effective People,

Free Press 1989, 2004.

Ilibaguza, Immaculee with Steve Erwin. Left To Tell, Accessible Publishing System, Pty Ltd 2008.

Martha A.S. Qorro, Zaline M. Roy-Campbell. Language Crisis in Tanzania, The Myth of English versus Education, Mkuki na Nyota 1997.

Mason, John. Know All Your Limits; then Ignore Them, Inside Publishing Group 1999.

Mason, John. An Enemy Called Average, NP 1990.

Maxwell, John C. Developing the Leader Within You, Thomas Nelson, Inc. 1993.

Maxwell John C. Talent Is Never Enough, Thomas Nelson 2007.

Nyerere, Julis K. Freedom and Development, Oxford University Press, 1968.

Nyerere, Julius K. Freedom and Unity, Oxford University Press, 1966.

Nyerere, Julius K. Our Leadership and the Destiny of Tanzania, African Publishing Group 1995.

Petruk, B. G. Julius Nyerere Humanist, Politician, Thinker, Mkuki na Nyota 2006.

Simonton, Dean K. Why President Succeeds: A Political Psychology of Leadership, Harvard University Press, 1984.

Websites

Biomed Central: www.biomedcentral.com

Daily newspaper: http://www.dailynews.co.tz

Haki Elimu: http://www.hakielimu.org

International Atomic Energy Agency: http://www.iaea.org

IPP Media: www.ippmedia.com

Ministry of Energy and Minerals: http://www.mem.go.tz

Ministry of Health: TB and Leprosy: http://www.moh.go.tz

Mwananchi Newspaper: http://www.mwananchi.co.tz

National Electoral Commission: http://www.nec.go.tz

Raia Mwema Newspaper: http://www.raiamwema.co.tz

TACAIDS: http://www.tacaids.go.tz/

TANESCO: http://www.tanesco.co.tz

Tanzania National Website: http://www.tanzania.go.tz/

This Day Newspaper: www.thisday.co.tz

TRA: http://www.tra.go.tz/

Medical Women Assct. of Tanzania: http://www.mewata.org

www.ingramcontent.com/pod-product-compliance
Lightning Source LLC
Chambersburg PA
CBHW020615300426
44113CB00007B/652